Adventures in Interpretation:
The Works of Hartmann von Aue and Their Critical Reception

Editorial Board

Literary Criticism in Perspective

James Hardin (*South Carolina*), General Editor

Stephen D. Dowden (*Brandeis University*), German Literature

Benjamin Franklin V (*South Carolina*), American and English Literature

Reingard M. Nischik (*Konstanz*), Comparative Literature

* * *

About *Literary Criticism in Perspective*

Books in the series *Literary Criticism in Perspective*, a subseries of the series *Studies in German Literature, Linguistics, and Culture*, and *Studies in English and American Literature, Linguistics, and Culture*, trace literary scholarship and criticism on major and neglected writers alike, or on a single major work, a group of writers, a literary school or movement. In so doing the authors — authorities on the topic in question who are also well-versed in the principles and history of literary criticism — address a readership consisting of scholars, students of literature at the graduate and undergraduate level, and the general reader. One of the primary purposes of the series is to illuminate the nature of literary criticism itself, and to gauge the influence of social and historic currents on aesthetic judgments once thought objective and normative.

Adventures in Interpretation:
The Works of Hartmann von Aue and Their Critical Reception

*Illumination of Hartmann von Aue from the
Große Heidelberger Liederhandschrift
(Heidelberg Universitätsbibliothek, cpg. 848, f. 184v).*

Will Hasty

Adventures in Interpretation
The Works of Hartmann von Aue and their Critical Reception

CAMDEN HOUSE

Copyright © 1996 by
CAMDEN HOUSE, INC.

Published by Camden House, Inc.
Drawer 2025
Columbia, SC 29202 USA

Printed on acid-free paper.
Binding materials are chosen for strength and
durability.

All Rights Reserved
Printed in the United States of America
First Edition

ISBN:1–57113–031–4

Library of Congress Cataloging-in-Publication Data

Hasty, Will.
 Adventures in interpretation: the works of Hartmann von Aue and their critical reception / Will Hasty.
  p.   cm. -- (Studies in German literature, linguistics, and culture. Literary criticism in perspective)
 Includes bibliographical references and index.
 ISBN 1-57113-031-4 (alk. paper)
 1. Hartmann von Aue, 12th cent.--Criticism and interpretation. I. Title.   II. Series: Studies in German literature, linguistics, and culture (Unnumbered). Literary criticism in perspective.
 PT1535.H37 1995
 831'.21--dc20

95-14520
CIP

For Isa and Nati.

Contents

Preface	xi
1. Introduction: The Scholarly Adventure	1
2. Hartmann's Life and the Chronology of His Works	11
3. The *Klage* (Complaint) and the Lyrics	23
4. *Erec*	36
5. *Gregorius*	52
6. *Der arme Heinrich*	68
7. *Iwein*	79
8. Conclusion: A Return to Points of Departure?	96
Works Consulted	101
Index	119

Acknowledgments

I would like to express my gratitude to the interlibrary loan department of Smathers Library at the University of Florida for its expeditious and friendly assistance during the completion of this volume and to the editors of the series *Literary Criticism in Perspective* for the opportunity to occupy myself with Hartmann.

W.H.
September 1995

Preface

IN RECENT YEARS the name and works of Hartmann von Aue have not been confined to university libraries. A 21 November 1983 story in *the Christian Science Monitor* discusses an English translation of Thomas Mann's *Der Erwählte* (*The Holy Sinner*), which is based on Hartmann's *Gregorius*. Siegbert Prawer's review of Ernst Pawel's life of Franz Kafka (24 June 1984; *The Washington Post*) refers to Hartmann's "exquisite sense of moral dilemmas and his marvelously subtle use of the rhythm, sounds and semantic resonances of the German language," with which Kafka may well have been familiar. A 29 December 1992 story in *La Stampa* discusses the debut of *La leggenda di San Gregorio*, "a play written in the twelfth century by a German monk(!), Hartmann von Aue." The name of Hartmann figures prominently in the recent book on medieval culture and history by Joachim Heinze, which is reviewed in the 26 November 1993 issue of the *Süddeutsche Zeitung*. In the same journal on 8 January 1995, a recent play by Tankred Dorst is discussed: *Des Zauberers neue Kleider*, which is based on Hartmann's *Der arme Heinrich*. All of Hartmann's narrative works, with the exception of the *Klage*, have appeared in English translation, and some (*Erec* and *Iwein*) are available in several recent and readily available English editions.

In the academy Hartmann continues to enjoy considerable attention. The high number of scholarly monographs and articles in both German and English indicates on both sides of the Atlantic a strong interest in the medieval author that shows no signs of abating. Despite the great number of these scholarly publications, or perhaps because of it, there is as yet no book that devotes itself primarily to the presentation of an overview of the critical literature. Readers of German can turn to two studies of Hartmann that serve as excellent introductions. Peter Wapnewski's book, which was originally published in 1962 and had appeared in seven editions by 1979, provides a solid introduction to Hartmann's works, although its conclusions are dated and in many cases contested. Christoph Cormeau and Wilhelm Störmer's 1985 book, *Hartmann von Aue: Epoche, Werk, Wirkung*, is the most recent and, hence, the most critically informed general introduction to Hartmann's works. Both of these books deal with previous critical literature, but their primary goal is not an overview of the critical literature itself. Such an overview is the goal of the present volume, which is also intended to serve as a general introduction in English to the works of Hartmann. The book is aimed at advanced undergraduates and beginning graduate students with some knowledge of medieval history, although I hope that more advanced graduate students and even specialists in the area may derive some benefit from the survey of critical literature and my approach to it.

In order to avoid clutter, the titles of secondary works (and the places of publication) are listed only in the chronologically arranged *Works Consulted* section at the end of the book. References to secondary works in the chapters themselves consist of the name of the critic, the date of her or his work, and the page(s) involved. Information that is not clear from the context is cited parenthetically. Since this book is designed for the use of readers who may not know the German of Hartmann or that of his modern German critics, I have provided English translations for most quotations from the primary and secondary German texts. Translations are my own unless otherwise stated. In some cases, where the original text may be of special value to readers of German in transmitting the flavor of an appraisal or interpretation, the original German has been cited preceding my translation.

The chapters on Hartmann's longer narrative works consist of two sections. The first section, which is intended primarily as an introduction to the respective work, includes a brief discussion of the manuscripts in which the work is preserved, the work's sources, its genre characteristics, its structure, and, finally, the broader literary traditions and the social, political, and cultural developments with which the work has often been connected. The second section deals more directly with the ways in which the work has been interpreted by critics over the decades, focusing in particular on the hero's development. According to the aim of the series *Literary Criticism in Perspective,* of which this volume is a part, secondary works are cited chronologically, whenever it is feasible, so that the reader can perceive the manner in which criticism evolves over the years. This book presents one possible selection and ordering of the available critical literature. Many other manners of selecting and ordering this literature are, of course, possible. The focus in the survey of interpretations, as stated, is on the idea of the heroes' development or progression, however conceived, whether such interpretation proceeds more or less directly from the plot or involves some conception of structure. This is an appropriate focus for a volume directed at a general audience, but it should be observed that it would also be valid and profitable to focus on the importance of nineteenth- and twentieth-century philology for Hartmann criticism, the painstaking textual criticism that resulted in the standard editions upon which the interpretations cited in this book are based, and/or on the vast amount of critical literature dealing with Hartmann's style and formal artistry: his employment of the four-stress rhyme couplets in his longer narrative poems, or his employment/alteration of the verse patterns of Old French or Provençal lyrics. The focus taken in this book, which is limited in its cursory treatment of significant areas such as these, is further limited by the impossibility of doing full justice to the vast amount of interpretive literature dealing with the idea of development in Hartmann's works. Even if significant interpretations have been omitted or have received less attention than they deserve (I have confined myself for the most part to published books and articles in major scholarly journals), it is hoped that the studies cited and discussed in this book provide an accurate and useful introduction to Hartmann's works and to major trends in their critical reception. I have attempted, to the best of my ability, simply to describe the contending positions, confining my own assessment to brief remarks at the end of each chapter. The reasons for this procedure will become clear in the Introduction: here I would say simply that a more descriptive approach to the rich diversity of the critical literature corresponds more closely to my critical perspective than an approach which assumes that all issues can and should be decided on the basis of a single critical school of thought (e.g., that which asserts moral didacticism as the primary goal of Hartmann's works). At the end of the book, the reader will find bibliographical information on the primary works cited in this book and on other significant editions of Hartmann's works, the Works Consulted section which lists secondary studies chronologically, and a section containing useful reference works.

1: Introduction: The Scholarly Adventure

THERE IS NO perspective from which the vast amount of critical literature dealing with Hartmann von Aue falls neatly into place. Only the broadest of trends are identifiable. The beginning point of modern critical interest in Hartmann is difficult to establish. After editions of Hartmann's works had appeared in the first half of the nineteenth century (*Der arme Heinrich* by Jakob and Wilhelm Grimm in 1815; *Iwein* by Georg Friedrich Benecke and Karl Lachmann in 1827; *Gregorius* by Lachmann in 1838; and *Erec* by Moriz Haupt in 1839; the songs and the so-called *Büchlein* [little books; the second little book turned out to be by another author, the first little book is also known as the *Klage*] by Haupt in 1842), articles and monographs dedicated to the edition and/or scholarly appraisal of his works began appearing in larger numbers (notably in journals such as the *Zeitschrift für deutsches Altertum* [1841-] and the *Zeitschrift für deutsche Philologie* [1869-]). It is in studies such as these that one might identify the beginning point of the literary criticism dealing with Hartmann's works.

Although one can artificially designate the mid nineteenth century as the starting point of Hartmann criticism, the works of Hartmann had already enjoyed a long history of reception previous to this time. If one overlooks the sixteenth-century Humanistic preoccupation with medieval German literature (the publication by Melchior Haiminsfeld Goldast of some of the minnesongs), one might say that medieval German authors such as Hartmann began to play a distinct role in modern literary criticism during the eighteenth century, close to the southwestern German region where many of these authors, including Hartmann, had once lived and worked: in the Switzerland of Johann Jakob Bodmer and Johann Jakob Breitinger. Bodmer and Breitinger were responsible for the appearance of Hartmann's lyrics in *Sammlung von Minnesingern aus dem schwäbischen Zeitpuncte* (Collection of Minnesingers of the Swabian Period, 1758–59). This publication caused something of a literary fashion among poets such as Johann Wilhelm Ludwig Gleim, Ludwig Christoph Heinrich Hölty, and Johann Heinrich Voß, who wrote minnesongs in Halberstadt and Göttingen, one of the breeding grounds of Germanic philology. A younger friend of Bodmer, Christoph Heinrich Myller, also published Hartmann's *Der arme Heinrich* and *Iwein* in the first volumes of his *Sammlung deutscher Gedichte aus dem 12. 13. und 14. Jahrhundert* (Collection of German Poems from the 12th, 13th, and 14th Centuries, 1784). Inspired by Myller's publications, Gerhard Anton von Halem published a verse rendition of Hartmann's *Iwein* in 1789 titled *Ritter Twein* (this spelling of the hero's name, obviously based on a misreading, was already contained in Myller's edition). A reprinting of Halem's poem, along with a critical introduction to it and to an anonymous 1789 essay titled "Von dem ritterlichen Heldensänger Hartmann von Owe, aus dem 12ten Jahrhundert," is provided by Beutin and Beutin (1994).

Bodmer and Breitinger's interest in medieval German poetry can be viewed as an aspect of their debate with Johann Christoph Gottsched, the premier arbiter of literary matters, about the appropriate constitution of the German literary language and, consequently, of the standard German language, for which the literary language provided the model. Within this debate the Middle High German works of authors such as Hartmann were enlisted in the service of a conception of literature that stressed, against the rationalistic France-oriented classicism propagated by Gottsched, the importance of provincial and archaic traditions and of poetic fantasy for literary language. The role played by Middle High German literature in this debate anticipates in many respects the Romantics' fascination with this literature and their questioning of Enlightenment thought, although Bodmer and Breitinger, as has been pointed out by Schulte-Sasse (1988, 36–37), were themselves, despite their valorization of fantasy, still very much advocates of Enlightenment. The period in which Bodmer and Breitinger labored did not provide the kind of support for medieval German literature that would be present in the early nineteenth century. According to the Enlightenment view of history as a constant improvement of the human condition, medieval works were inevitably considered inferior and only of antiquarian interest. Frederick the Great, to whom Myller's books were dedicated, responded to the gift of these volumes with an appraisal of the medieval works, which is presumably valid for Hartmann's *Der arme Heinrich* and *Iwein*, that was perhaps not untypical of its age:

> You judge much too highly of the poems of the 12th, 13th, and 14th centuries, the publication of which you have expedited, and which you consider so useful for the enrichment of the German language. In my opinion they are not worth the powder of a single musket shot. They did not deserve to be pulled out of the dust of oblivion. At any rate, I would not tolerate such miserable stuff in my own collection of books but would rather throw it out.

As instructive as such negative reactions to the medieval works is the fact that Bodmer and Breitinger could consider them to be compatible with their aesthetic and critical interests. Hartmann's major works, as later scholars would recognize, were in most cases very deliberate reworkings of French sources; thus, they seem to be poorly qualified to play a role in a conception of literature stressing poetic fantasy, at least as this was understood in the eighteenth century. However incorrect or inappropriate this use of medieval literature may seem, it nevertheless had constructive consequences, to the extent that it was linked to Bodmer and Breitinger's polemics against Gottsched's "rule dogmatism" (Schulte-Sasse, 36) and, beyond this, to the enrichment of the German poetic idiom with words — *Brünne* (coat of mail), *Degen* (thane), *Fehde* (feud), *Hain* (grove), *Hort* (hoard), *Recke* (warrior) — that Enlightenment advocates of East Middle German such as Gottsched rejected as provincial and archaic.

Romantic readers and critics of the early nineteenth century — often erroneously cast as the modern discoverers of medieval German literature (Beutin and Beutin 1994, 9–10) — had what might be seen as a similarly productive (mis)understanding of Hartmann and of medieval literature more broadly. In the rising nationalistic fervor of the Napoleonic years, readers found in his works a specifically German attitude, an expression of what were considered straightforward German values, such as courage and loyalty. Works such as *Der arme Heinrich* were seen as demonstrative of German-ness in the same manner as the *Nibelungenlied:* the selfless devotion of the unnamed peasant girl in Hartmann's tale became the female counterpart to the unswerving manly resolve of Hagen. Beginning with the late Romantics (for Schulte-Sasse after 1807–8 [1988, 170]), the German courtly works of the High Middle Ages provided a way of discovering one's own aspirations in another age, of viewing oneself as a member of a community with roots that reach back into a mythical prehistory. Proponents of this approach to the medieval works preferred not to see what later critics would point out: social solidarity in the Middle Ages was based not on national qualities that in later centuries were perceived to distinguish French from Germans, but rather primarily on social class. Nobles, even those who spoke different languages, moved among their peers throughout Europe, sharing the same tastes and pastimes (among which was the sponsorship and enjoyment of literature). Isolated from his pan-European aristocratic context, Hartmann — in the same way as Wolfram von Eschenbach and the *Nibelungenlied* — came to be viewed as prototypically German. The momentum of this nationalistically toned Romantic appraisal of Hartmann was not slowed by the greater historical awareness of appraisals such as that of Gervinus, who found it lamentable that works such as those of Hartmann were the "products of a closed class of people and of a limited time" and that they could not, therefore, have a general value and attraction for the peoples of later ages (1853, 367). Notably, this historically critical appraisal did not prevent Gervinus himself from adopting a more Romantic posture in his rejection of those courtly works that seemed to him more overtly conventional (the Arthurian works) and in his embrace of those (particularly *Der arme Heinrich*) which "miraculously" managed to grasp, in spite of the pervasive conventionality he perceived in medieval literature, some timeless human quality (368–9).

Throughout the nineteenth and into the current century, the critical reception of medieval literature in general, and thus of the works of Hartmann in particular, remained very much influenced by the late Romantic appraisal. For this reason most nineteenth-century German critics were not prepared to deal with Hartmann's works as conventional, constructed texts that were the more or less direct reworkings of other texts (in the majority of cases French). Literary critics from the Romantics to the Naturalists, and artists such as Richard Wagner, preferred to see in the works of Hartmann and of other medieval German authors — whenever it was possible to do so — the unmitigated and spontaneous outpouring of creative energies grounded in the spirit, blood, and soil of the German people. It is perhaps fortunate that the works of Hartmann, with the possible exception of *Der arme Heinrich*, were protected to some extent from this Romantic (mis)understanding precisely because they were perceived as more conventional. While this undoubtedly affected the status of Hartmann vis-à-vis poets such as Wolfram and works of the heroic-epic tradition (the *Nibelungenlied, Kudrun*), with the former appearing to be less of a poet, it perhaps permitted the works of Hartmann to pass into the current century with less ideological baggage. One has the impression that critics of the later nineteenth century were able to devote themselves to Hartmann only by ignoring or arguing against appraisals such as that of Wilhelm Scherer, who viewed Hartmann as a "translator" who "hid his individuality" (1883, 186). The impression seems to be confirmed by the fact that the folk-oriented literary history of Bartels, despite its ideological differences from Scherer, also regards Hartmann as a "translator" and mentions this medieval author only in passing in its introduction (1905, 47).

I have been using the term *(mis)understanding* because it is important to recognize that the late Romantics' appraisal of medieval court literature, however questionable some of its basic assumptions may seem, may have had positive effects to the extent that it was connected to the productive energy at the heart of the intensive philological preoccupation with medieval German literature — the efforts of Benecke, the brothers Grimm, and Lachmann are most notable — that resulted in the first critical editions of Hartmann's works (notably, the famous edition/translation of *Der arme Heinrich* of 1815, which was undertaken by the brothers Grimm with the motive of outfitting Hessian volunteers against Napoleon, and Lachmann's 1827 edition of *Iwein*, which has been viewed as the beginning point of serious philological preoccupation with medieval texts) and in the introduction of the medieval works in High German translation to the general population. If these philologists had possessed a greater sensitivity for the international social milieu in which authors like Hartmann von Aue lived and worked and for the "constructedness" of the courtly works, it seems likely that they would not have devoted so much time and energy to producing critical editions that recognized and endeavored to minimize scribal errors and alterations in the manuscripts, and to making many medieval works (particularly the *Nibelungenlied,* and *Der arme Heinrich* in the case of Hartmann) popular beyond a narrow circle of intellectuals and critics. However historically arbitrary it may seem today, the conception of poetry as a spontaneous creative outpouring of the German spirit might be seen as inseparable from the establishment of the textual foundation upon which the subsequent critical reception of Hartmann was based.

Much of the critical literature from the latter half of the nineteenth century to the present day can be seen not merely as an attempt to grasp Hartmann and his works in historically adequate terms, but also as an attempt to deal with the late Romantic legacy, to modify, correct, or reject critical approaches to Hartmann and his works that are characterized by an unhistorical subjective intimacy, lyricism, spontaneity, and German-ness. Not untypical for critical appraisals in the latter nineteenth century is Pfeiffer's transparently Romantic praise of Hartmann on the basis of the author's "Liebenswürdigkeit, Innigkeit, Seelenkenntnis und Gemütstiefe" [amiability, intimacy, knowledge of the mind, and depth of feeling] (1859, 8). Nearly a century later Nordmeyer voices the following opinion: "Of what good are the most subtle psychological distinctions, when there is no documentation whatever of the existence of the person to whom they refer? One must proceed from criticism of the text itself, and not from an image of the poet-human that is made on the basis of unsystematic impressions" (1942, 279). Applying a term usually employed with reference to the literary works to literary criticism itself during the decades separating these two critics, one might speak broadly of a scholarly *quest* for structure. One observes that the nationalistically toned element of subjective intimacy in portrayals of Hartmann and his works gradually begins to recede as critics of the latter nineteenth and early twentieth centuries increasingly attempt to appraise them systematically within some broader objective framework.

This quest for structure was complex and uneven, often combining revolutionary insights with abiding traditional assumptions. Studies such as those of Schmid (1874) and Schreyer (1874) viewed Hartmann as a medieval version of the Romantic poet, his lyrics as the highly subjective and frequently tormented outpourings of a man involved in a number of unhappy relationships with hard-hearted women. Not too many years later, insights into the conventionality of Hartmann's lyrics were made by Saran (1889), who refuted the idea that these lyrics could be understood as *songs* in the modern sense of the word (a single idea developed from the beginning to the end). Stylistic analyses were frequently motivated by the wish to praise Hartmann at the expense of Chrétien de Troyes (Gärtner 1875; Jeske 1909) on the basis of criteria such as the former's German depth and the latter's Gallic superficiality. During the same time, the textual foundation was being solidified in less overtly ideological studies of style and form such as those of Selisch (1884), Henrici (1885), Zwierzina (1893 and 1901), Hagen (1895), Erdmann (1896), Schroeder (1896), Gierach (1917), and Naumann (1918). Despite the impression that criticism of Hartmann during these years was still tapping around in the darkness of a largely unexplored field, it was in studies of Hartmann's use of the infinitive (Monsterberg-Mückenau 1884), of the monologue as a structuring principle (Peetz 1911), of Hartmann's manner of describing living creatures (Heyne 1912), and of Hartmann's dualistic Weltanschauung (Langer 1913), that more consistently objective criteria for the appraisal of Hartmann's works began to be established. Notable in view of its ongoing importance for future criticism was the detailed study by Schönbach (1894), which differed from most of the others of this period both in the detail of its analysis and by suggesting that religious literature and sermons provided the source material and inspiration for much of Hartmann's work. Schönbach's study was the most extensive and significant of the latter nineteenth century, and it was perceived as a model by his contemporaries (Martin 1896). Critics were not only becoming more familiar with Hartmann's works, their formal characteristics (cf. Muth's study of Middle High German meter, 1882, and Vos's study of Hartmann's diction and rhyme technique, 1896), and the period in which they were composed in studies of a broader cultural orientation (Schultz 1879); they were also developing a sensitivity for the often haphazard way in which Hartmann's works had been preserved over the centuries, and hence for the inevitable constructedness of standard editions of the author's works. (The editing of Hartmann's works, which began in the nineteenth century and continues to the present, might be seen merely as the latest phase in their transmission through the centuries, a phase that is largely shaped by changing editorial criteria; such a change is contained in Okken's attempt [1970] to describe the transmission of Hartmann's *Iwein* on the basis of a statistical and diagrammatic method, rather than by establishing a genealogical tree, which was the preferred editorial procedure subsequent to Lachmann). A culmination of the early phase of Hartmann criticism, which was more concerned with the philological task of establishing sources than with interpreting the works, might be seen in the two volume study by the Dutchman Hendrik Sparnaay (1933/38). This study actually suggests two different frameworks for understanding Hartmann's works, the first being the life of the author: Sparnaay's study is billed as a biography, and it establishes something resembling a life story for Hartmann on the basis of his works. The second framework is a philological analysis of possible relationships between the works of Hartmann and oral and literary traditions from antiquity to the Middle Ages. Sparnaay's biography is a seminal study that presents a comprehensive view of Hartmann's works from which criticism to this day has benefited. It also shared some earlier assumptions (e.g., that it is possible to establish Hartmann's biography on the basis of his works) that were to become increasingly problematical in subsequent decades, when Hartmann's life and his works were subjected to an increasing number of contending interpretations. During this time Sparnaay continued, sometimes stridently (1952, 1965), to defend his view of Hartmann's life and the chronology of his works.

From the perspective of the conceptions of structure that began to appear in the thirties and forties, many of the earlier studies, however accurate and fruitful for future interpretation, still seemed to be intuitively groping toward a coherent understanding of Hartmann and lacking an appropriately objective interpretive framework. Two such conceptions endeavored to free the critical evaluation of Hartmann from some of the unsound notions of the previous century and to ground the author's works in intellectual currents of the Middle Ages. The first, represented especially by the study of Ittenbach (1937), based the meaning of Hartmann's works not on events at the level of plot, but rather on the combination of longer narrative segments. Significant in this approach, in which the literary work is often portrayed as a cultural analogue to the Gothic cathedral, was not the story of the hero, the interpretation of which invited the arbitrariness of modern readers, but rather the number of narrative segments in a given work and the manner in which they were assembled. The task of the modern reader is, for Ittenbach, to arrive at an appreciation of structural and numerical symmetry, for which the Middle Ages presumably had a much greater sensitivity and in which the primary meaning of the work rested. For Eggers, who followed Ittenbach's kind of analysis, this structural principle represented a principle of "objective certitude" (1956, 93); it also enabled the critic to overcome weaknesses he saw in approaches to Hartmann that based themselves on plot or content (*Inhalt*), rather than on form (7). Number symbolism as defined by critics such as Eggers was rejected in later studies (Linke 1968, Heinze 1973) that nevertheless accepted and perpetuated the basic idea of the overriding importance of a structure that consists of a greater or lesser number of narrative segments that are identifiable on the basis of differing criteria.

The other major structural conception, represented by Kuhn's article on Hartmann's *Erec* (1948), was grounded in medieval Christian thought. In this conception the two-part structure of many of Hartmann's works, which had been recognized but never convincingly explained by earlier critics, was seen as corresponding to the moments of prefiguration and fulfillment in Christian typology (although originating in patristic biblical exegesis, this correspondence is seen by Kuhn as a broader medieval form of thinking that would have left its mark on all literature): the second structural segment is anticipated by and completes the first according to the same typological form of thinking that regards the New Testament as anticipated by and completing the Old. Thus, the coherence of Hartmann's works is not based on a logic of linear progression (e.g., that of modern psychology) at the plot level; rather, it is established in a jump, a disjunction, a moment of transcendence corresponding to Christ's act of redemption that connects parts of the story at the structural level. This structural conception, which prevents — or at least is supposed to prevent — the adventures of Hartmann's heroes from being viewed in terms of a nineteenth-century notion of *Bildung,* has been of immense importance in Hartmann scholarship to the present day, with critics such as Voß (1983) arguing that criticism has yet to fully grasp its implications for the understanding of Hartmann's works.

Building upon and in some cases modifying or rejecting the assumptions of these two influential interpretive models, which ground the meaning of Hartmann's works in broader conceptions of structure, a veritable explosion of interpretations in recent decades has deepened the historical and cultural understanding of Hartmann's works and imparted to the critical discussion of them an ever-increasing disciplinary and interdisciplinary diversity. Although characterizations are difficult, due to the great variety of interpretive interests and conclusions, one broad trend nevertheless seems to be observable. Whereas the movement of criticism during much of this century has been away from the perceived arbitrariness of a subjective, historically uninformed approach, toward the secure knowledge seemingly held forth by some broader objective structure, there has been a tendency in recent decades to adopt what might be considered a more strictly subjective approach to Hartmann and his works. Such a tendency is visible in increasing skepticism about whether prevalent objective conceptions of structure are really able to overcome subjective arbitrariness rather than merely to transfer it to a different level (Wiehl [1974] has questioned the valorization of narrative segments in studies such as Linke's; Voß [1983] has criticized what he sees as the modern subjective biases still at work in interpretations based on Christian typology). It is visible in the increasing willingness to base interpretation on events at the plot level rather than on some broader notion of structure and to stress the importance of that with which the heroes begin in contrast to that which they are generally seen to acquire. Finally, this turn is visible in doubt about whether a purely objective understanding of Hartmann and his works, assuming such an understanding is possible, would be of any interest or relevance to modern readers, who somehow manage to enjoy his works even if they know little about the Cluniac reform, early Scholasticism, or Gothic architecture. The words of Clark describe a critical approach that does not endeavor to deny or conceal its subjective orientation:

> The existence of a text over time of necessity engenders varying, and often equally valid readings. We read medieval texts in the twentieth-century because they speak to us, albeit differently than to the audience of the twelfth and thirteenth centuries, with voices that are nevertheless penetrating and true to us now. We approach texts with a mixed perspective, so that our knowledge of the Church Fathers is tempered with a belief that many fundamental aspects of human nature remain constant over time. (1989, 6)

The postulation of varying and often equally valid readings, corresponding to the different interests of modern critics, suggests the presence of two tendencies in interpretation, one that is oriented toward grasping its material (Hartmann's works) according to some objective (medieval) criteria and another that inevitably sees its material according to its own interests and priorities, which are also generally those of some broader (modern) interpretive community. In contrast to the approach of many early critics and readers of Romantic inclinations, many recent critics of a more consciously subjective orientation have benefited from the awareness of the constructedness of Hartmann's works that has been achieved in this century, and they have perhaps begun to take this awareness to another level by recognizing the seemingly inevitable constructedness (i.e., the values/interests/assumptions) of their own interpretations.

My view of the criticism of Hartmann von Aue as a *scholarly adventure* is based on the assumption that interpretation is both discovery and creation and thus is something like the adventurous activity of Hartmann's Arthurian heroes: an individual (critic/knight) discovers an unknown, provocative Other and proceeds to make sense out of it, or to give structure to it, according to some idea about the way things are or should be. In the adventure of interpretation, the Other is experienced not as a dragon or giant, but rather as some aspect of a work or a group of works that provokes because it does not fit into any of the available critical models as presently conceived. This moment of discovery sets in motion the attempt to grasp this new aspect, to adapt ourselves to it and it to us in such a way that it becomes meaningful. The general trends of criticism outlined above, when exemplified in greater detail, will, I believe, uphold the perspective outlined here: early understandings of Hartmann's works, characterized in large part by a nationalistically toned subjective immediacy, gradually give way to interpretations that mediated, or contextualized, critical understanding of Hartmann's works in various ways; these contextualizations have in recent decades been supplemented, and in some instances modified or criticized, by interpretations that seem to be placing emphasis on the subjective element in criticism without necessarily renouncing the claim to objective validity. Continuing the Arthurian analogy, the literary criticism of Hartmann von Aue has, like Erec and Iwein in their adventures, appropriated and become familiar with a strange territory, perhaps in the end also to discover itself. Hartmann von Aue criticism can be considered a scholarly adventure: the validity of this perspective, which is also obviously a hypothesis, is demonstrated, I believe, by letting the critical literature speak for itself.

2: Hartmann's Life and the Chronology of His Works

ALONG WITH WOLFRAM von Eschenbach and Gottfried von Straßburg, Hartmann is considered one of the three great poets of the literary efflorescence occurring in Germany in the latter twelfth and early thirteenth centuries. Although he composed no single work on the same scale as Wolfram's *Parzival* or Gottfried's *Tristan*, Hartmann is justifiably regarded as "medieval Germany's most influential writer" (Thomas 1982, 1). One the main reasons for this is his versatility: Hartmann excelled in a variety of genres, including Arthurian works, works of a more legendary type, and love songs. In his works Hartmann makes no references to Wolfram and Gottfried, whereas they both mention Hartmann in their works. Their postures toward Hartmann indicate that he was considered by his contemporaries to be one of the most important poets of the day. Despite some passages in Wolfram's *Parzival* that indicate an attitude of more or less aggressive competition with Hartmann, Wand argues that Wolfram is interested above all in participating in and continuing the Arthurian narrative that Hartmann introduced to Germany (1989, 207) and that the apparently aggressive posture Wolfram frequently appears to adopt toward his predecessor is not a programmatic personal attack, but merely furthers Wolfram's narrative aims.

Admiration of Hartmann is articulated in the famous literary revue contained in Gottfried's *Tristan:*

> Ah, how Hartmann of Aue dyes and adorns his tales through and through with words and sense, both outside and within! How eloquently he establishes the story's meaning! How clear and transparent his crystal words both are and ever must remain. (Citing Hatto's translation [1960, 105]).

Hartmann was regarded as a seminal figure who was praised as a model and emulated by poets during his lifetime and throughout the thirteenth century. The influence of Hartmann has been noted in the works of Wirnt von Grafenberg, Heinrich von dem Türlîn, Konrad Fleck, Rudolf von Ems, Ulrich von Türheim, Der Pleier, Konrad von Würzburg, and the authors of *Der jüngere Titurel, Gauriel von Muntabel,* and *Wigamur.*

Despite his literary importance there are no known historical documents of his existence. This is not unusual, since there is — besides the oft cited documentation of an allowance to the famous lyricist Walther von der Vogelweide for the purchase of a coat — no known extraliterary reference to any of the great poets of this period. Consequently, what is known about Hartmann has to be based on his literary works, on references, such as the above-cited passage from Gottfried's *Tristan,* made about him in the works of other medieval authors writing around the same time, and on highly stylized visual representations of the author in illustrated manuscripts of the thirteenth century. Among the many obstacles presenting themselves to the biographical interpretation of this material, two are especially difficult. First, the manuscripts of many of the works were produced many years, in some cases centuries, after their original composition by the author. The only complete manuscript of *Erec,* for example, is contained in the Ambraser manuscript, which was produced in the early sixteenth century, some three centuries after the author's death. Changes were inevitably made during this long period of the work's transmission, as scribes made errors and interpolations of various kinds, so that it is impossible to say with certainty today whether all the verses in current standard editions of this work are attributable to Hartmann. Although *Erec* is perhaps the most extreme case, the same problem holds true to a greater or lesser extent for all of Hartmann's narrative works, and certainly for the lyrics (some strophes transmitted under his name are not considered to be those of Hartmann), none of which has survived in its original form — assuming there ever was such a form, rather than several different working versions. Second, any statements by Hartmann about himself in his literary works, assuming they can with some certainty be attributed to him and are not interpolations, were made during a time of transition from oral to written literature when authors were beginning to insert themselves into their own stories in the form of the fictional persona of the narrator. They probably did so not to transmit information about their private lives, although it is possible that they did so coincidentally, but rather to further their literary designs. Consequently, it is in many cases difficult to disentangle the historical Hartmann from the literary Hartmann, who has been stylized to serve some literary purpose or other (this problem is explored in detail in the 1980 study of Arndt). The difficulty of disentangling the historical Hartmann from the narrator figure in his works suggests that the attempt to do so may be anachronistic: if the author's life outside of literature had been important to a medieval audience's understanding of his works, one might expect more information about the author's life to have survived.

Due to these and a multitude of other problems, there are no certain answers to the most basic questions about the poet: When and where did Hartmann live? Who was (were) his sponsor(s)? Where did he achieve the education of which he speaks in the prologues of *Der arme Heinrich* and *Iwein?* Did he participate in a Crusade, or in two, as some of his lyrics suggest? Who was the lord whose death possibly resulted in Hartmann's turn from worldly Arthurian works to works of a spiritual concern, and possibly also in participation in a Crusade? In what order did he write his works? Answers to questions such as these have been inextricably bound to the manner in which the literary works themselves have been interpreted. The lack of historical data with which to ground a view of the author's life in extraliterary history seems to guarantee that Hartmann's life and career will be posited as much as they are discovered, that the view of them will be determined at least in part by the historical and methodological presuppositions of the respective critic. A creative element in reconstructing the life story of Hartmann is indicated by the wide variety of characterizations of Hartmann. Although the majority of scholars have, with Jong (1964), viewed Hartmann as strongly didactic and moralistic, he has also been seen, according to the specific interests of the respective critics, as a practical man who was antagonistic toward art as escapism or mere entertainment (Thomas 1982), a humorist (Kuttner 1978), a man possessing little fantasy (Saran 1889), a skilled creator (Clark 1989), a translator (Firmery 1901), a combination of classicist and enthusiast (Halbach 1939), a spokesperson for feudal-aristocratic values (Fischer 1983), and a miserable failure as a poet (Witte 1929).

Hartmann's works, as we shall see, allow for many different interpretations and, consequently, for many different views about the author's life, interests, and concerns. In the Hartmann criticism of the latter nineteenth century, when the understanding of the author's life was largely connected to the interpretation of his lyrics, critics did not doubt that Hartmann's self-references could be taken at face value. Assuming that Hartmann employed his lyrical language in the same manner as Johann Wolfgang von Goethe and Romantic poets, these critics constructed life stories for Hartmann that were rich in detail, describing, for example, the number and kind of amorous relationships in which Hartmann was involved (most saw one or two lengthy affairs, although some also perceived more casual liaisons, and others, such as Heinzel [1872], pondered three lasting relationships). As the importance of broader literary and cultural traditions and of the accidents and mistakes involved in literary transmission and scholarly editing was increasingly appreciated, the specifics of Hartmann's life became less immediately accessible, and scholars began to base their views more cautiously on the few scraps of seemingly unambiguous information about Hartmann's life and the chronology of his works that the works themselves seem to provide. Many studies have resulted, which, although sharing certain basic assumptions, present a variety of difference in the detail of Hartmann's life story.

In *Der arme Heinrich* Hartmann refers to himself as a *dienstman;* this designation means that he belonged to the unfree class of *ministeriales,* a heterogeneous social group consisting of functionaries, administrators, and servants who performed duties of various kinds at the larger courts of the German kings and princes. In the prologues of *Iwein* and *Der arme Heinrich,* Hartmann calls himself a *rîter* [knight] who can read and write. During this age an education could only be obtained under the auspices of the church, in a cloister or a cathedral school. Hence, sometime during his youth, perhaps before entering the service of his feudal lord(s) and literary patron(s), Hartmann may have lived among monks and received teaching in the liberal arts, although the assumption of an early religious education has not gone unquestioned: Müller states that Hartmann did not attend a religious school during his youth, but rather learned to read as an adult from clerics. Müller further posits that a knightly author such as Hartmann could not have possessed the skills to write the poems himself and that he consequently dictated them to clerics trained in book production (1974, 7–10). Based on his assumption of the Zähringer as Hartmann's patrons, Mertens looks for monasteries in the territories of this ducal family that might come into question as the place of Hartmann's early education. The most probable monastic setting for Hartmann's education would have been St. Georgen, which was open to young men of Hartmann's unfree status (1978a, 162), although Mertens prefers the hypothesis that Hartmann studied in a cathedral school, in which case that of Mainz was the most likely (164). If he studied in such a school, then Hartmann would have known Latin. Hartmann's knowledge of some of the works of Chrétien de Troyes (Keller states that he "only rarely errs" in his translation of *Erec et Enide;* 1987, vx) also makes it highly probable that he knew French. Based on verses in his *Klage,* in which the allegorical figure of the heart speaks of the magical *krutzouber* (magical herb) that it has brought back from *Kärlingen* (France), it has been thought that Hartmann may have spent some time in France. While it cannot be ruled out and would be entirely consistent with what is known about Hartmann's life and works, a stay in France cannot be proved on the basis of this passage.

The language of Hartmann's works indicates he is of Alemannic origin, that he probably came from a region that today encompasses southwestern Germany, northern Switzerland, and the French Alsace. Hartmann's Alemannic origin is also supported by the words of the later medieval author Heinrich von dem Türlîn, who refers to this region when he says of Hartmann that he was: "von der Swâbe lande" [from the land of the Swabians]. Numerous suggestions have been made about the precise location of Hartmann's literary activity within this large region in which there are many places with the name *Aue*. Three of these were mentioned by Schmid (1874, vi-vii), who himself argued for the last: 1) since the author was depicted in two *Minnesang* manuscripts with a coat of arms resembling that of the Wespersbühl house, it was assumed that he might be located among the servants of this family on the island of Reichenau; 2) it was suggested that Hartmann belonged to a house that was in the service of the Zähringer family and that he lived close to Freiburg; 3) Hartmann might also have lived on the upper Neckar, close to Württemberg. Schreyer's discussion from the same year also lists these three possibilities before advocating another: Hartmann was not a Swabian at all, but rather a Frank. Consequently, one would have to look further to the north, in a completely different geographic region, for Hartmann's home. This supposition is based on a problematical passage in one of Hartmann's Crusade songs (*Des Minnesangs Frühling* [MF] 218,19–20): "und lebte mîn her Salatîn und al sîn her / dien braehte mich von Vranken niemer einen vuoz" [If Saladin and all his army were alive, / they wouldn't bring me a foot from the land of the Franks]. These lines, among the most interpreted verses in all of Hartmann's works, have yielded a great variety of different meanings both with respect to Hartmann's home and to his possible participation in a Crusade. In a recent article (1990) Wis suggests that *Vranken* does not mean the kingdom of the Franks in Germany, but rather the Frankish kingdom of Jerusalem (the *Regnum Francorum Hierosolymitanum*). Whatever Hartmann may have meant in this passage, the majority of scholars considers it unlikely that the poet intended to say he lived and worked in Frankish territory. Yet another Swabian location that has been suggested is Eglisau, in the northern part of the canton of Zurich. This location has been supported by Sparnaay (1933, 13) and more recently by Thomas (1982, 1).

In recent years critical attention has turned from the attempt to pinpoint Hartmann's home to the identification of his patron. This identification, which would simultaneously provide important information about Hartmann's home, is to some extent facilitated by a consideration of the material preconditions for a literary career such as that of Hartmann. Manuscripts of source works, such as those of Chrétien de Troyes, had to be obtained; the expense of parchment and the financial support of scribes and authors had to be paid. The activity of an author such as Hartmann could only be supported by a rich and powerful lord and patron with high-level connections to the nobility beyond Germany. In the region suggested by the linguistic characteristics of Hartmann's works, there would appear to be only three families that would have been in a position to support an author such as Hartmann: the imperial Hohenstaufen, the Welfs, and the Zähringer (Mertens 1978a, 32–34, Cormeau and Störmer 1985, 45). It has been tempting to link Hartmann and his works to the first of these, the imperial family, and thus to bring Hartmann into a more immediate contact with the major events and undertakings of the day. Following Schweikle (1979, 256–59), Wis (1990) argues that the Hohenstaufen emperor Frederick I ("Barbarossa") is the lord whose death Hartmann mentions in MF 218,19; since Frederick died in June 1190, Hartmann may have written these verses during the Crusade that began under Barbarossa in 1189, in which Hartmann possibly participated. Others believe that the Zähringer were Hartmann's patrons. Following the study of Müller (1974) in this respect but offering more detailed and compelling arguments, Mertens (1978a) puts forward the Zähringer Bertold IV and/or Bertold V as Hartmann's patrons. The lord of whose death Hartmann sings may be the former, who died in 1186. This would also indicate that Hartmann's Crusade songs refer to his possible participation in the expedition of 1189. Further support for Mertens's argument that the Zähringer were Hartmann's patrons is provided by visual representations of the author contained in the Große Heidelberger and the Weingartner song manuscripts, which depict Hartmann with a coat of arms consisting of white eagles' heads on a blue or black background. This coat of arms is similar to that of the Wespersbühl family in Thurgau as of 1238, although it is more likely that it is a variation of the Zähringer coat of arms, which it also resembles. It is also possible that artists, who rendered the coat of arms many years after the author's death, simply invented one. More useful information about Hartmann may be contained in *Der arme Heinrich,* whose protagonist is named Heinrich von Aue. Most scholars have considered this similarity of names too striking to be merely coincidental: "It would be a remarkable coincidence if Hartmann wrote a legendary story about an Aue who came from the same area [i.e., Swabia] but was not related to him" (Mertens 1978a, 156). Heinrich, who is at the beginning of Hartmann's work a rich and powerful noble, marries the daughter of a peasant at the end of the work. In the Middle Ages marriage tended to be a matter of political alliance rather than personal preference; a good marriage could bolster the fortunes of a family for generations, while a bad one could result in a loss of social status. The rough outlines of Hartmann's own family history may be discernible in the events described in *Der arme Heinrich:* the Aues may once have been a family of free nobles who fell into feudal servitude (that is, into the *ministeriales*). This servitude may have been the result of a bad marriage (Sparnaay 1938, 2), but it is more likely that the fairy-tale wedding at the end of *Der arme Heinrich* is merely the poetic transfiguration of whatever may have been the real reasons for the fall of this family into servitude (Mertens 1978a, 162). While there are many references to historical Heinrich von Aues, Mertens considers that the poor Heinrich in question may be connected to the family of a Heinricus de Owen (or Owon) that lived in the early twelfth century in Au bei Freiburg, although it is unlikely that this historically documented figure is identical with Hartmann's protagonist. Several factors are cited by Mertens in support of the connection of Hartmann to Heinricus de Owen and of both to the ducal house of the Zähringer. First, this house pursued its agricultural aims by granting a high degree of freedom to the peasants in its territories. Such a freedom corresponds to the favorable situation of the peasant with whom Heinrich seeks refuge in Hartmann's work (Mertens 1978a, 156). There are also some indications that the family of Aues to which Heinricus de Owen (and possibly also Hartmann) belonged was originally free, but that it fell during a time of increasing centralization of power into the servitude of the powerful Zähringer (Mertens 1978a, 156–57). Finally, the Zähringer had connections to the patrons of Chrétien de Troyes and thus would have been in a position to provide Hartmann with the sources for his Arthurian works. Although Mertens has made the most compelling case to date, it is not yet possible to say that there is a consensus with respect to the identity of Hartmann's patron.

The most significant event in the life of Hartmann may have been his participation in a Crusade. Because of songs such as MF 218,5 ("Ich var mit iuwern hulden"; I take leave from you now) that depict Hartmann's departure on a Crusade, many critics have endeavored to identify the Crusade in which he participated and to place this in relation to other developments posited for the author's life. Many consider that Hartmann took part not in the Crusade of 1189 under the leadership of Barbarossa (either in the emperor's service or in that of the Zähringer), but rather in the one of 1197 that was led by Barbarossa's son Heinrich VI. This supposition is based on the controversial passage MF 218,19–20, which is cited above. If read as it appears in the manuscripts, then one must conclude that Saladin was dead at the time the song was composed. Since the famous sultan of Egypt and Syria who had reconquered Jerusalem in 1187 died in 1193, this would suggest that the expedition to which Hartmann refers in this song was that of 1197. Jacob Grimm and Hermann Paul, however, considered that editorial intervention ("und lebt' mîn herre, Salatîn und al sîn her") is necessary to restore the line to its original form, in which case the song yields a different understanding: "If my lord were still alive, then Saladin and his entire army would not bring me a foot from the Kingdom of the Franks." According to this reading, Saladin was still alive, and the Crusade in which Hartmann participated was the earlier one, possibly as a consequence of a spiritual crisis brought about by his beloved lord's death. Such a crisis is sometimes employed to establish the chronology of Hartmann's narrative works: at about the same time that Hartmann began to turn away from the worldly service of ladies in *Minnesang* toward service of God in the Crusades, the author might also have turned away from the worldly concerns of Arthurian romance (i.e., *Erec* and possibly the first thousand verses or so of *Iwein*) toward the more overtly spiritual concerns in *Gregorius* (Kuhn 1953, 79–81; Pastré 1989, 191). Such a theory provides support for placing *Gregorius* immediately after *Erec* and for dating its composition in the late 1180s. Participation in the later Crusade does not seem to leave enough time for such a spiritual development, since the participation in a Crusade, and the composition of *Gregorius, Der arme Heinrich,* and *Iwein* would have to be pressed into the years between 1197 and circa 1205. Despite fierce debate about the meaning of these lines (Sparnaay 1965), there is increasing skepticism among scholars — given the variety of possible meanings, depending on the editorial criteria applied — that the lines concerning Saladin will ever provide unambiguous support for a crisis in Hartmann's life, for his participation in the earlier or later Crusade, or for the chronology of his works (Cormeau and Störmer 1985, 31). It should be noted that MF 218,19–20 is only one of many passages in Hartmann's works that are used to garner support for the earlier or the later Crusade or for both.

There is no record of Hartmann's birth or death. An approximate determination of them is based on the chronology of his works. A beginning point for establishing when Hartmann lived and worked is a passage from another literary work, Wolfram von Eschenbach's *Parzival*. To illustrate the consequences of a rowdy knightly tournament he has portrayed, Wolfram makes an extremely rare allusion to a historical event: "Erffurter wîngarte giht / von treten noch der selben nôt: / maneg orses fuoz die slâge bôt" [The vineyards at Erfurt still show the effects of trampling from the feet of many a horse]. Thanks to this offhand comparison between Wolfram's fictional knightly tournament and the historical conflict at Erfurt in 1203 between two rivals for the crown of the empire, Philip von Schwaben and Otto IV, it is likely that Wolfram's work was composed around 1205. In an earlier section of *Parzival,* a reference is made to *Iwein,* which for stylistic reasons is presumed to be Hartmann's last work. Hence, all of Hartmann's works were likely written before the year 1205. These passages in Wolfram's work provide the only absolute chronological point of reference (Cormeau and Störmer 1985, 26–32). It is impossible to say whether Hartmann lived beyond 1205 or whether he produced other works after *Iwein* which have been lost. Gottfried's *Tristan,* which is dated around 1210, mentions Hartmann as still alive, while Heinrich von dem Türlîn's *Diu Crône,* written around 1220, laments his passing. This suggests that Hartmann died between 1210 and 1220, although the apparent lack of works subsequent to *Iwein* from so prolific an author suggests an earlier rather than a later date for his death.

Establishing the approximate year of his birth and the beginning of Hartmann's literary activity is much more difficult. *Erec,* which is presumed to be among Hartmann's first works, contains a reference to fur coats from a place called Connelant (verse 2003) or Ikonium, a Saracen sultanate the territory of which now lies in Turkey. Although seeming to provide evidence for a dating of *Erec,* the meaning of this verse is as puzzling as all the others that seem to hold forth information about the relation of Hartmann's works to their historical context. Fur coats from Ikonium have been termed "an impossibility of natural history" (Rosenhagen 1917, 301–2). Based on his assumption that the mention of Connelant refers to the conquest of this city in 1190 during the Crusade undertaken by Barbarossa, Sparnaay assumes that Hartmann's Connelant verses were not written before this year (Sparnaay 1933, 7). If Hartmann was about twenty years old when he composed *Erec,* and if *Erec* was indeed among his first works, this would mean that he was born sometime between 1160 and 1170. Fourquet (1934) suggests that Hartmann's use of *Connelant* may be a misunderstanding of the Old French word for rabbit skin and that it does not, at any rate, suggest a familiarity on the part of Hartmann and his audience with the city of Ikonium. Wis posits much more recently that Hartmann's Connelant is for the author as well as his audience "a geographically vague, distant fairy tale land like Arabia or India" (1990, 403), combining real knowledge with popular fantasy, and that it is probable that Hartmann came to know of Connelant after diplomatic contacts were established between its sultan Kildisch Arslan and Frederick I in 1173 (Wis 1991, 278), at which time the colorful emissaries of the sultan made quite an impression on the western Europeans. If Hartmann had been present at a festival held by Frederick for these guests from the East, he might have personally witnessed the same kind of events that we find in literary form in the festival at the court of Arthur upon the marriage of Erec. Based on this possible connection, Wis argues that *Erec* was composed around 1180, if not even earlier (1991, 278). This implies an earlier birth of Hartmann, perhaps closer to 1160. The beginning and end of Hartmann's literary career, and by extrapolation the approximate dates of his birth and death, are thus generally seen as marked by the Arthurian works *Erec* and *Iwein.*

Establishing the order in which Hartmann's works were written has been based primarily on stylistic criteria, according to the idea that works demonstrating a greater formal coherence and control of language were written later than ones that seem rougher and less polished. A concrete example of the stylistic criteria used to establish the chronology of the works is the initial line of *Der arme Heinrich* ("Ein ritter sô gelêret was"; a knight so learned was) and that of *Iwein* ("Ein ritter, der gelêret was"; a knight, who was learned). Zwierzina (1901) had argued that the relative clause of the *Iwein* verse ("der gelêret was)" indicates a higher degree of linguistic perfection than the seemingly ungrammatical verse from *Der arme Heinrich*, thus indicating the former work was written later. Schirokauer (1951/52b) undermined this argument by asserting that the word *sô* in the initial verse of *Der arme Heinrich* should be understood as a relative pronoun, in which case it would not be linguistically inferior to the *Iwein* verse. Neumann (1956) seems to undermine both arguments by pointing out that one cannot be sure in either case if the manuscripts, which are often faulty, present Hartmann's original text. The article of Grosse (1961/62), which provides an overview of these and other arguments with respect to these verses, itself posits that the Hartmann's use of language in the entire prologue of *Iwein* is "freer and more sovereign" (194), which indicates that *Der arme Heinrich* was the earlier work. The works sometimes provide more explicit clues. In the *Klage,* for instance, Hartmann refers to himself in the initial verses as a *jungelinc* (young man); this, combined with other features that demonstrate what is apparently a still unfinished and inexperienced author, leads most scholars to place the composition of the *Klage* at the beginning of Hartmann's career alongside, if not previous to, that of *Erec. Gregorius,* on the basis of its stylistic characteristics, is seen as closer to *Erec,* with *Der arme Heinrich* preceding *Iwein.* Some critics posit that approximately the first one thousand verses of *Iwein* were written before *Gregorius.* This position garners support for the idea of a spiritual crisis on the part of Hartmann, the idea being that Hartmann began composing *Iwein* immediately after concluding *Erec* but interrupted his work on this Arthurian work and turned to poems of a religious kind on the death of his lord. This thesis was originally put forward by Zwierzina (1898) on the basis of stylistic criteria (Hartmann's use of rhyme), continued by Schröder (1957), and has been recently argued by Pastré (1989), who considers that this thesis is generally accepted today (190), although it has in fact been contested by many scholars (Cormeau and Störmer 1985, 26). The dates of composition of *Gregorius* and *Der arme Heinrich,* just as is the case with the chronology of the songs, cannot be established with certainty, although a significant difference in stylistic quality seen by some scholars between *Gregorius* and *Der arme Heinrich* suggests a relatively longer period between the composition of these two works (Cormeau and Störmer 1985, 31). Based on the assumption of increasing literary ability on the part of their author, the longer narrative poems were likely written during the last two decades of the twelfth century in the following order: the *Klage* and *Erec* (around the same time), *Gregorius, Der arme Heinrich,* and *Iwein.* Many if not all of these works may have been written in the final decade of the twelfth century and the initial years of the thirteenth century, as postulated by Scherer (1883) and Sparnaay (1933); or, if the arguments recently put forward in the articles of Wis are accepted, then Hartmann's career began earlier, perhaps around 1180. While it is difficult to establish the exact time frame, the order of the works as stated above, which was originally put forward by Lachmann, is accepted by the majority of scholars (cf. Barthel 1854, 31; Grosse 1961/62, 194; Linke 1968, 156; Heinze 1973, 257; Wiehl 1974, 302; and Thomas 1982, 1). The assumption underlying this chronology is succinctly stated by Sparnaay: "Every work represents an advance over the previous one, so that the scrutiny of Hartmann's formal artistry provides the best means of determining the relative chronology of the various works" (1938, 80).

A noteworthy criticism of the endeavor to base the chronology of Hartmann's works on stylistic criteria is the study of Bürck (1922), which received little attention among later scholars. Depending on criteria and on examples chosen, Bürck argues, any order of the works is conceivably possible; *Erec* might be placed after *Iwein* on the assumption that the greater number of "uncourtly" words seen in the former would have made it richer and more colorful for Hartmann's knightly audiences (11–12). Bürck doubts that medieval authors such as Hartmann would have been very concerned about their rhymes being pure in neighboring dialects. Perhaps most important, Bürck sees Hartmann first and foremost as the representative of a knightly culture and the speaker of a knightly language characterized by a high degree of uniformity (Bürck cites nineteen of the most frequent rhyme combinations in the courtly romances [26] and points out that Hartmann uses, on the average, one of these for every seven of his couplets; it is nothing more or less than the great uniformity of his language that makes him, for Bürck, the courtly author as which he is typically seen). Although few scholars today will agree with all of her positions, Bürck puts forward an entirely different framework for evaluating the chronology of Hartmann's works, one that is grounded in the knightly language and milieu of the twelfth century rather than on possibly modern conceptions of style and artistic development.

A prominent idea with respect to the songs is that the Crusade lyrics were written after the courtly love songs (this will be exemplified in the next chapter). Although this idea is plausible, it nevertheless makes the chronology of the songs dependent on a criterion — a gradual development from worldly to spiritual values on the part of Hartmann — which may in fact be foreign to the literary situation in which Hartmann worked. The "romanticized image of the poet" underlying this conception of the lyrics chronology is pointed out by Cormeau and Störmer (1985, 27).

Would it be a mistake to see such a romanticized image of the poet at the heart of the commonly accepted chronology of Hartmann's works? Much like the author's heroes, who begin their careers unformed, gain initial recognition and honor before a period of crisis, and then achieve lasting honor in a more selfless and spiritual approach to the world, Hartmann begins his literary career with a work, *Erec,* that on many accounts does not go beyond a reaffirmation of the worldly values of Arthurian knighthood (Eroms 1970, 158; Schröder 1972, 310), proceeds with two works of a more spiritual tone (*Gregorius* and *Der arme Heinrich*), possibly as the result of a spiritual crisis provoked by the death of his lord, and culminates in the crowning achievement, *Iwein,* which is characterized by a literary conception that recovers the originally lacking spirituality and places it in a proper relationship to worldly concerns. Although the similarities are broad, it is difficult to avoid seeing in appraisals of Hartmann's career a dynamic that resembles the one often seen in his heroes' adventures. If the same dynamic is present in both areas of scholarship, then it would seem that there may be reasons for the generally accepted chronology of Hartmann works other than a gradual increase in formal and linguistic skills, reasons that may have as much to do with a modern idea of linear, incremental development as with the historical context of Hartmann's works. The presence of such an idea would not in itself invalidate this chronology, but it would seem to suggest that, within a differing framework (e.g., the greater strength of youth as opposed to the declining faculties of old age), the better works might be understood as the earlier ones.

3: The *Klage* (Complaint) and the Lyrics

THE *KLAGE* AND the lyrics have often been treated together, for both share a preoccupation with love, and it was long thought that both are documentations of Hartmann's amorous life outside of literature. As the conventional nature of the longer verse poem and the songs has become increasingly clear, the connection to Hartmann's life outside of literature has become more uncertain. The *Klage* is preserved only in the Ambraser Heldenbuch (Österreichische Nationalbibliothek, Vienna; cod. Vind. ser. nov. 2663), a large parchment manuscript containing twenty-five works by Hartmann (*Erec* and *Iwein* are also included) and other authors that was commissioned by Emperor Maximilian I and completed by his secretary Hans Ried of Bozen between 1504 and 1516. The poem appears under the following title added by Ried: "Ein schöne Disputatz. Von der Liebe. so einer gegen einer schönen Frawen gehabt und getan hat" (A Beautiful Disputation about the Love that Someone had for a Beautiful Woman). The title *Das Büchlein* (the little book), which some scholars still use to designate this work, is based on an error by its first editor, Moriz Haupt, who mistakenly associated this poem with another poem in the Ambraser Heldenbuch, which he called *Das zweite Büchlein*. It was later determined (by Saran 1898 and Kraus 1898) that the latter work was not by Hartmann. The author himself refers to this poem as a *klage*. As is the case with *Erec,* this is the only preserved manuscript of this work, indicating that this was not one of Hartmann's more popular works.

The source of the *Klage* is unknown. The poem shows similarities to the Provençal and French traditions of the *complaintes d'amour,* or *saluts* (a kind of love letter). Piquet pointed out similarities between this work and the Old French poem *Un samedi par nuit* [One Saturday at Night] (1898, 73–98), positing this was one of Hartmann's sources. The *Klage* may also be related in some way or other to a disputation with quite a different focus, the *Visio Fulberti, Dialogus inter corpus et animam* [Vision of Fulbertus, A Dialogue between Body and Spirit], a widely disseminated text in which the disputation occurring between the body and the soul involved establishing responsibility for their damnation (cf. Sparnaay 1933, 56–61 and Wapnewski 1962, 38).

The *Klage* is considered to be Hartmann's first longer work. Like all of Hartmann's longer narrative poems, it is composed in four stress rhymed couplets, except for the final part (from verse 1645), when a crossing rhyme pattern is employed. The poem takes the form of an allegorical disputation between personifications of the *herz* [heart] and the *lîp* [body] of a *jungelinc* [youth] named Hartmann, and it consists of four parts. In the first (verses 1–484, according to Haupt's edition), the body reproachfully addresses the heart for forcing it to seek the love of a lady who repudiated it. As a result the body has suffered unending torment and has lost its desire to continue living. In the second part (verses 485–972) the heart responds that the body shares responsibility for falling in love, since it was through the eyes of the body that the image of the beloved reached the heart. The heart also chastises the body for not pursuing the lady's love with greater diligence and provides some advice: "swer ahte hât ûf minne / der darf wol schoener sinne" [whoever values love must refine himself]. During the third section of the poem (verses 973–1644), which is a dialogue between the heart and the body, the advice of the heart to the body culminates in the *krûtzouber von Kärlingen* [magical herb from France], which is a means of achieving the love of God and of one's fellow man. The *krûtzouber* consists of *milte* [friendliness], *zuht* [restraint], *diemut* [humility], *triuwe* [loyalty], *staete* [constancy], *kiuscheit* [modesty], and *gewislîchiu manheit* [dependable manhood] mixed in a heart without hatred. The body promises to avail itself of the *krûtzouber* and is sent back to the beloved lady to renew the suit in the fourth and final section of the work (verses 1645–1914).

This poem has been considered one of Hartmann's most independent achievements (Piquet 1898, 73–76), and Wisniewski (1963) has even made the claim that its definition of love as an ennobling and ethically beneficial force separates the high courtly period from early courtly literature (for which Veldeke is cited as the paradigm), in which love was typically little more than an affliction to be endured (251). Although expressing a similar positive appraisal, Wapnewski also speaks of a "pallor of thought and occasional deficiency in logical execution" that is indicative of "the lack of resources of the beginner" (1962, 39). This view, whether justified or not, may help to explain why the *Klage* has received little scholarly attention in comparison to Hartmann's other works.

The first detailed study of this poem was that of Schönbach (1894), who suggested that the dialogue between the body and the heart might be understood as a legal disputation. Schönbach based himself here on similarities between Hartmann's poem and legal codices such as those of the Saxons (the *Sachsenspiegel*) and the Swabians (the

Schwabenspiegel). This view was later criticized for ignoring that legal terminology is frequently found in colloquial speech and does not by necessity imply a legal situation (Piquet 1898, 73–98) and for seeming to require the instance of a judge that is not present in the poem. The *Klage*, just as the *saluts* upon which it was likely based, was possibly directed to a beloved lady, according to Sparnaay (1933), although it is not possible to determine who this inspiring lady may have been. In the French work *Floire et Blancheflor*, Sparnaay points out, the lovers send each other "letres de salus et d'amors" [letters of greeting and love] (56). For Sparnaay it is almost certain that this work was not a private letter in the modern sense but was intended for public presentation and that in this poem Hartmann transmits his own conception of *minne*, which avoids the erotic dimension in favor of a more ascetic ideal of service, although the youthful poet is still much influenced by his source and was not yet able to add much to it (54–57).

Prominent has been the idea that this disputation between body and heart is a secularized version of the kind of theological debate between the body and the soul that is found in theological texts such as the *Visio Fulberti*. Ehrismann, for example, saw in Hartmann's poem "a secularization of the spiritual dialogue between soul and body . . . consequently an adaptation of a spiritual theme to the worldly Minne doctrine" (1927, 155). In a similar appraisal Wapnewski speaks of this work in terms of a *Profanierung* [making profane] of the religious themes of the body/soul disputations (1962, 38). This antithetical, if not dualistically toned approach, which at least implicitly opposes a courtly heart to a theological soul, has been countered by other scholars, who have pointed out that the role of the heart is entirely compatible with many of the theological conceptions of Hartmann's age. Citing numerous examples from patristic literature, Wisniewski demonstrates that the heart is portrayed not only physically as a bodily organ, but also symbolically as the hidden center of wisdom and thought (1963, 239–40). Reviving Schönbach's thesis that the poem rests on a legal foundation, Wisniewski argues that it is both an *Anklage* [legal accusation] and a *Wehklage* [a complaint], containing elements of legal terminology couched in the literary genre of the *complaintes d'amours* in such a way as to resemble the bipartite structure of *Erec* as pointed out by Kuhn (Wisniewski, 235–37). In his book length study of this poem, Gewehr (1975) continues Wisniewski's assault on the idea that the *Klage* represents a courtly antithesis to theological literature by undertaking to demonstrate that its descriptions of the attributes of the heart are entirely consistent with central ideas of early Scholasticism. Hartmann's *herz*, according to Gewehr, is the center of man's rational forces and is able to experience only what is delivered to it by the bodily senses (259). Gewehr sees here an indication of Hartmann's close familiarity with the Aristotelian orientation of the early Scholastics, which he may have obtained in a childhood education in a cloister or cathedral school. For Mertens also, the *Klage* is not to be seen in dualistic terms as a secularized version of religious conceptions, but rather as a purely immanent ethical treatise that is shaped both by the moral teachings of classical antiquity and the ideals of contemporary vernacular literature, particularly Old French and Provençal (1988, 19).

The article of Grosse (1981) differs from most of the other critical appraisals, both in its cursory treatment of the relationship of the *Klage* to the theology of Hartmann's day and in its high assessment of the importance of this poem for all of Hartmann's works. Grosse posits that Hartmann's first work establishes a secular foundation for the discussion of amorous relationships between men and women. Although this foundation remains "indebted to God" (35), it has been largely detached from its "spiritual/theological associations" and defines a courtly concept of life that affirms the things of the created world. It is upon this foundation, established by Hartmann's initial poem, that Hartmann's subsequent works — all of which deal in some way or another with *minne* — will build.

Perhaps the most central problem in the appraisal of the *Klage*, that concerning the exact relationship of worldly to spiritual values, is one that we shall see again in scholarship dealing with Hartmann's later and longer narrative works. Here as elsewhere, fundamental assumptions about the intellectual and spiritual climate in which Hartmann worked shapes modern appraisals of his works. Thus, Hartmann's age was "despite all harmonizing and gradualistic tendencies basically dualistic" (Wapnewski 1962, 38), or, conversely, it was pervaded by the harmonizing spirit of Scholasticism (as set forth in Gewehr's study), thus lacking "a dualistic, ascetic orientation" (Wisniewski 1963, 238). A point upon which most scholars agree, despite such differences, is that the *Klage* transforms love into an ennobling force. The teaching of the work is succinctly put by Wisniewski:

> a man overcome by the power of love must not remain in a state of ease, but rather must overcome the weakness and indolence of his body, so that he can, by means of actions of ethical worth that increase his own value, become worthy of love and thus achieve bliss. (1963, 246–47)

Seiffert and Jackson have recently made this general interpretation socially and politically more concrete. Seiffert argues that Hartmann's *Klage* deals with an issue at once aesthetic and moral: to understand how a courtier recognizes and acknowledges his distinctive but nevertheless subservient place "in a social framework informed not only by relations of inequality, but also by the exercise of authority and power" (1988, 49); Jackson sees the ideology of love service manifested in this work as "a transference into the amatory sphere of the feudal relationship of service and lordship as it may have been seen from the lower end of the feudal hierarchy by a young serving knight . . ." (1994, 178). Offering an appraisal that is concerned neither with religious values nor with political implications, Clark sees in this poem an early anticipation of Hartmann's more general concern with mind. *Die Klage*, in Clark's view, "sets out an anatomy of the functions of mind as the seat of both reason and emotion, and as an entity capable of reflection, imagination, and problem-solving" (1989, 44).

The lyrics attributed to Hartmann were organized into eighteen songs by Karl Lachmann and Moriz Haupt in *Des Minnesangs Frühling* (originally published in 1857; the thirty-seventh revised edition by Hugo Moser and Helmut Tervooren appeared in 1982; specific songs are designated according to the song numbers [in Roman numerals] and according to the strophe and verse numbers from Lachmann and Haupt's original edition). Strophes of Hartmann's songs are transmitted in the three major codices containing minnesongs which were all assembled around 1300: sixty strophes in Die große Heidelberger (or Die Manessische) Liederhandschrift (Universitätsbibliothek, Heidelberg; cpg 848), ten strophes in Die kleine Heidelberger Liederhandschrift (Universitätsbibliothek, Heidelberg; cpg 357), and twenty-eight strophes in Die Weingartner Liederhandschrift (Württembergische Landesbibliothek, Stuttgart; cod. HB XIII 1). Hartmann's authorship of some of the preserved strophes is doubted; seven strophes attributed to Hartmann appear under the names of Reinmar and Walther von der Vogelweide in other manuscripts. The number of strophes and their order differs from one manuscript to another.

In the critical history of Hartmann's works, the appraisal of his lyrics has perhaps experienced the most radical transformation. Originally seen as reflections of events in the author's life, as we shall see in some detail below, the songs today tend to be seen as belonging to a highly conventional lyrical tradition in Germany with roots both in French and Provençal lyrics and in indigenous lyrical traditions. Contemporary criticism rarely sees the *Minnesang* tradition as grounded in individual experience. As Brackert has pointed out in his 1983 translation of selected minnesongs (259–76), *Minnesang* presents a strongly ritualized and rigidly conventional portrayal of the relationship between man and woman. It is not private experience, but rather a *Gesellschaftskunst* [a communal art form] based above all on formal virtuosity and mastery of roles and codes shared by the singers and their audiences. One of the conventional situations in these lyrics is that of the so-called *hohe minne* [high minne], in which the singer/knight heaps praise upon and swears eternal love, loyalty, and service to a lady who nevertheless typically treats him with cruelty and scorn; despite this adversity, or because of it, the singer/knight presumably refines and ennobles himself (it has become clear in recent studies [cf. Kaplowitt 1986] that this particular convention in the lyrics may not be as central as once thought). Brackert provides a brief overview of the different manners in which critics have attempted to deal with *Minnesang* over the years: 1) critics have focused on connections between *Minnesang* and other literary traditions such as goliardic poetry, classical Latin literature, and Arabic love lyrics; 2) *Minnesang* has been linked, on the basis of its frequent idealized portrait of the lady, to cult worship of the Virgin Mary; 3) the lyrics have, finally, been seen as based on social, feudal dynamics: the singer and the idealized lady who rejects him but whose service he cannot and will not leave may be a sublimated expression of the feudal relationship between the socially inferior class to which the singers belonged and the position of power occupied by the lord and lady of the castle, the singers' patrons. The latter approach to the lyrics, which has perhaps enjoyed the most vibrant discussion in recent decades, is represented in different ways by the studies of Elias (1939), Köhler (1970), Peters (1973), and Liebertz-Grün (1977), each of which receives a brief review in Brackert's afterword. Kaiser has presented a similar appraisal of the significance of the Arthurian works (1973).

Hartmann was also certainly familiar with and influenced by other German lyricists of his day, such as Hausen, Morungen, Reinmar, Fenis, Meinloh, and many others (Sparnaay 1933, 44–45), but it is also likely that some of these singers were influenced by the lyrics of Hartmann (Blattmann [1968] posits for example the influence of Hartmann on Reinmar). Given the difficulty of establishing the chronology of the songs, the order of influences is difficult to establish. Recently, Sayce (1988) has argued that Hartmann belongs to a second phase of the German lyric, which contains Romance features but no longer imitates specific Romance poems, a practice that had been common among the first lyricists in Germany (53). Sayce also posits a greater significance of the Romance (Provençal and Old French) influence and an attempt on the part of Hartmann to distance himself from native lyrical traditions (63).

The critical reception of Hartmann's lyrics has moved gradually from a view of the lyrics as expressions of individual experience to an understanding of them as part of a broader, highly conventional lyrical genre. Early critics understood Hartmann's songs literally. When, for example, Hartmann spoke of distance from his beloved, critics supposed that he was on a trip (for example to France, where he found the *krutzouber* mentioned in his *Klage* [cf. Saran 1889, 15–16]).

With time it was recognized that Hartmann's lyrics participated in a broader lyrical tradition with a limited number of recurring themes and images whose significance may have been figurative rather than literal: expressions of distance, to continue the example, might merely be an expression of the seeming unattainability of an ideal the poet has set for himself.

Even earlier critics such as Schreyer were aware of the difficulty of constructing biographical events on the basis of Hartmann's lyrics: "The songs offer in their somewhat general attitude not much evidence for the biography..." (1874, 14). Despite such realizations, most nineteenth-century critics, departing from a Romantic conception of the lyric as a language of subjective expression, considered that Hartmann's songs were a reliable instrument for assessing qualities of character particular to the author and for reconstructing events in his private life. Barthel concentrated on the author's character, positing that a streak of originality caused him to distance himself from most of the other contemporary lyricists, whose songs were characterized by a "schwärmerische unmännliche Empfindelei" [dreamy, unmanly sentimentality] (1854, 65). For Barthel the plaintive, submissive posture of many contemporary lyrics was offensive to Hartmann's masculine pride, even if it is possible that his aversion to this form of *Minnesang* was the result of a love affair that had gone sour (66).

Two studies from 1874 arrived at fairly detailed constructions of Hartmann's personal life. According to Schmid, Song I ("Sît ich den sumer truoc riuwe unde klagen"; Since I spent the summer in pain and lamenting), particularly MF 206,10–18, indicates that as a youth Hartmann had already loved a lady of high social standing. Because of a similar relationship described in Ulrich von Liechtenstein's *Frauendienst* [Service for Ladies], Schmid believed this lady was possibly one of the daughters of the lord of the castle with whom Hartmann might have come into contact as a youthful playmate (49). After becoming a young man, presumably after the death of his lord, which is documented by MF 206,14, Hartmann foolishly expressed his love for his erstwhile childhood playmate openly and was contemptuously rejected. This episode is portrayed in Song XV, MF 216,29, the so-called *Unmutston*, or "song of discontent," beginning with the verse "Maniger grüezet mich also" [many greet me in this way] (50). This outcome does not leave Hartmann bitter. He blames it on his own low social standing and courtly imperfections (Songs II ["Swes vröide an guoten wîben stât"; He who has joy from good women] and IV ["Mîn dienst der ist alze lanc"; My service has been much too long]). Nevertheless, the double blow dealt the youthful poet by the death of his lord and the rejection by his lady led him gradually to view worldly things with "indifferent eyes" (51), and eventually culminated in his participation in the Crusade of 1189, which is documented in Song V, MF 209,25 ("dem kriuze zimt wol reiner muot"; A true heart embraces the cross). Upon his return from this Crusade, Hartmann supposedly had acquired courtly manners (during a possible sojourn in Flanders or Brabant; 61) and learned how as a knight to acquire the favor of a lady (51). According to Schmid, a second love relationship began at this time. With this lady, to whom Hartmann directed his second *Büchlein* (which Schmid wrongly attributed to Hartmann), Hartmann enjoyed, despite the interference of the *huote* [lady's guardians; blocking figure(s)] a "virtuous relationship beyond reproach" (51). Frequent travel in the service of his lord, however, forced Hartmann occasionally to seek comfort in the arms of other women. It is by one of these other women that Hartmann is chastised because he cannot completely free his mind from his distant lady (Song IX, MF 212,37: "'Ob man mit lügen die sêle nert . . .'"; If one nourishes the soul with lies). After a few years had passed, Hartmann also participated in the Crusade of 1197, which is demonstrated by Song XVII, MF 218,5 ("ich var mit iuwern hulden, herren und mâge"; I take leave from you now, my lords and relatives).

Schreyer (1874) shares with Schmid the assumption that the songs and the two so-called *Büchlein* are the works that tell us the most about Hartmann's life, but his ideas about the events behind the songs are quite different and correspond more closely to the moralist for which Hartmann has typically been taken. Also relying on the model of Ulrich von Liechtenstein's *Frauendienst* (25), Schreyer sees in Hartmann's lady a member of his lord's family, possibly a daughter, and the *Unmutston* (MF 216,29) is likewise taken as a rejection of the young poet. In contrast to Schmid, Schreyer believes that Hartmann does not give up his service to this lady after this rejection. This relationship, which experienced "all kinds of vicissitudes, that would have stemmed from the whimsy of the beloved and mutual misunderstanding" (26), underlies all of Hartmann's love songs. The songs which suggest that Hartmann has sought love elsewhere (e.g., the *Unmutston*) are dismissed as jests (28,30). After returning from the Crusade of 1197, to which all of his Crusade songs are seen as referring, the poet finally found favor with his lady. Schreyer sees in this ultimately successful relationship not only an instance of the normal kind of *Minnedienst,* or love service, which by its very nature is supposed to be long and difficult for the knight (25), but also a more general paradigm: "even today it is not too rare that a previously spurned lover in the end is granted a sympathetic ear" (37).

The connection of the songs of Hartmann to events in his private life became more difficult as the formal characteristics of the lyrics began to receive closer scrutiny. It was increasingly recognized that what were previously understood as coherent songs were actually sequences of individual strophes, only some of which (e.g., the *Unmutston*) were seen as constituting *songs* in the modern sense of the word. Many "songs" revealed themselves to be combinations of strophes whose relationship to one another corresponded to a logic other than the gradual development of a single idea from beginning to end. An important study demonstrating the difficulty of applying a modern understanding of the lyric to the songs of Hartmann was that of Saran (1889), who systematically separated those strophes that might properly be considered as belonging together from the many individual strophes that had been erroneously (by Lachmann and Haupt) grouped together as "songs." According to Saran, Hartmann and his contemporaries stood between a more archaic stage (indicated by the frequent occurrence of individual strophes) and a more modern, polystrophic form of lyric. In recognition of this earlier historical phase in the development of the lyric, Saran suggests as a replacement for the word *song* the terms *strophic circle* or *strophic sequence,* which suggest that individual strophes were usually organized *kreisförmig* [in the form of a circle] around a central idea and only rarely according to the linear progression typical of the modern lyric (13). Saran's closer look at Hartmann's lyrics yielded some sober conclusions: "The same thought is repeatedly taken up and elaborated upon . . . the reason lies in the poverty of thought and lack of fantasy of our poet" (12). Although striking a blow at the coherence of the songs as traditionally understood and weakening the anachronistic view of Hartmann as a medieval version of the Romantic poet, Saran does not doubt that the poet's life and relationships can to some extent be reconstructed, if the arbitrary speculations of past studies (Saran specifically mentions Schreyer and Wilmanns [1869], who had posited two relationships based on his division of Hartmann's songs into two "song books") is given up and objective criteria employed, which for Saran are features of language and meter. Saran departs from strophe MF 218,5 ("Ich var mit iuwern hulden"), which shows, he believes, Hartmann's departure on the Crusade of 1189. Based on content, as well as on linguistic and metric characteristics (particularly the nature of the initial stress of verses), the chronology of the other songs is then established in relationship to this one. Similarly to his predecessors, Saran sees a real love relationship behind such strophes as MF 206,10 ("Ich hân des reht, daz mîn lîp trûric sî"; I am right to have the blues) and the *Unmutston* (MF 216,29). The announcement of the lady's rejection of his service in the former strophe must be true, reasons Saran, because it is juxtaposed to a factual event: the death of his lord (30). In contrast to Schreyer, the *Unmutston* is seen as serious and angry (16). In Song VIII, MF 212,13 ("Rîcher got, in welher mâze wirt ir gruoz"; Dear God, how will she greet me), Saran sees indications of the trip to France, which Hartmann also seems to suggest in his *Klage* (37).

Two tendencies in critical appraisals of Hartmann's lyrics become visible as skepticism about their biographical value increases. One observes an increasing recognition of the extent to which these lyrics belonged to and shared the language and concerns of a broader lyrical tradition with its own specific features, which do not vary greatly from one singer to another, and one also observes continuing attempts to link the lyrics to the life of Hartmann, not in the simple way it was done previously, but rather in terms of the individual imprint Hartmann may have made on the *Minnesang* tradition despite its conventionality.

In his discussion of Hartmann's lyrics, as in his discussion of Hartmann's other works, the seminal study of Sparnaay (1933) combines older and newer critical tendencies. Sparnaay questions the idea that the lyrics provide a means to reconstruct events in the author's life, taking aim at the notion that the lyrics are equivalent to an "activation of the erotic drive" (44), although some songs, such as 216,1 ("Swes vröide hin ze den bluomen stât"; whoever takes joy in flowers of the meadow) bring Sparnaay to concede the presence of more subjective, erotic elements. For Sparnaay the lyrics are part *Mode* [fashion] and part *Dienst* [service]: "The language of these poets is not the frivolous expression of hoped for pleasures, but a clever game of courtly entertainment" (46). In this game the poets hoped to obtain both *Lohn* [reward] and *Ehre* [honor] (44–46). For Sparnaay, Hartmann's *minne* is not so much love directed at specific ladies (although the wife of his lord may have been connected in some ways to his love service), but rather "the spiritual glorification of the ideal woman" or a "pretend love in the service of the court" (51). As with Saran, the only song allowing more concrete conclusions about events in Hartmann's life is 218,5 ("Ich var mit iuwern hulden"). In it Sparnaay sees a deeply religious Hartmann giving up a worldly love that leads to no concrete results in favor of a higher love of God as he departs on the Crusade of 1197 (51). If the Crusade songs were Hartmann's last, as Sparnaay believes, and if the Crusade in question was that of 1197, then the songs would have been composed in the period from 1187 to 1195 and would document in a general way Hartmann's gradual turn from the worldly love service of *Minnesang* to service of God in the Crusades, possibly as a response to the death of his lord and to the wish of his lord's widow that he not sing anymore of love (51–52). This last thesis indicates that the idea of a personal development documented by the lyrics has not been given up entirely, even if the postulation of specific relationships is no longer made with the assurance of the previous century. Sparnaay also draws attention to another problem: the preserved songs of Hartmann possibly represent only a fraction of his total production, so that even if a construction of his life were possible on the basis of his preserved lyrics, it would inevitably be incomplete (44).

Although solidifying the foundation of a more objective understanding of the lyric tradition in Germany in other articles (1936, 1968), Kuhn also perceives the individual mark made by Hartmann's love lyrics to be very pronounced (1953). In contrast to earlier negative appraisals (Saran, as we have seen, considered that Hartmann lacked fantasy and depth of thought [22], Sparnaay notes the lack of imagery in his songs [2]), Kuhn sees Hartmann as filling a role that is often reserved for the later poet Walther von der Vogelweide by positing for Hartmann's lyrics a process analogous to that which he sees in the author's epic works. Hartmann's conception of love becomes an "Anti-Minnesang" that emerges from a sense of personal guilt (i.e., *Schuld*) and turns resolutely against "jedes scheinbare 'Vorhandensein' des höfischen Tugendsystems der Minne" [every apparent "given" of the courtly love complex] (74), in much the same way as the adventures of Erec and Iwein subsequent to their fall respond to an apparently given, but ultimately illusory, condition of fame and honor. Hartmann, according to Kuhn, ultimately rejects *Minnesang* in two equally vehement ways, both of which reveal it to be mere *Schein* [illusion]: In the *Unmutston* (216,29), the poet turns to lowborn women to realize the experience of love, while in the Crusade songs the salvation of the soul is critically juxtaposed to the illusory, because insubstantial, worldly bliss of *Minnedienst* (74–75).

Continuing the assumption that the lyrics are indicative of a development on the part of Hartmann is Wapnewski, who speaks of a "seelische Entwicklung" (a spiritual development) and distinguishes four chronological phases in Hartmann's lyrical poetry (1962, 31–36). In the first phase Hartmann more or less directly emulates the conventions of the Provençal and German lyrical traditions that preceded him (e.g., "Ich muoz von rehte den tac iemer minnen" [215,14]; I must always love the day). This attitude shows the same uncritical acceptance of the conventions of courtly love that are visible in the *Klage*. The second phase is characterized by a loss of the feeling of joy stemming from love's ennobling power, which elsewhere in the *minne* tradition accompanies the pain of unrewarded service, and an increasingly critical attitude (e.g., "Nieman ist ein saelic man" [214,12]; no one is a happy man). The third phase of Hartmann's lyrical development involves what Wapnewski calls a rejection of *minne* based on "the spirit of practical reason." This rejection of a love that holds no promise whatsoever of fulfillment, which anticipates the songs of *niedere* (low) *minne* by Walther von der Vogelweide, is exemplified by the *Unmutston*. In Hartmann's Crusade songs Wapnewski perceives a final rejection of *minne* and of the worldly values propagated by the love and service of highborn ladies in favor of the love of God. Like Sparnaay before him, Wapnewski views the Crusade songs (for Wapnewski also it is the Crusade of 1197) as the last in Hartmann's lyrics, positing that there is no way back to the worldly lyric once this spiritual form of *minne* has been adopted.

The book on Hartmann's lyrics by Blattmann (1968) departs from an investigation of the relationship of MF 217,14 to Reinmar's MF 167,13 and ends by arguing on the basis of formal characteristics that all of Hartmann's songs, including all but one of the songs that had been declared by previous scholars as spurious (Blattmann thinks MF 214,42 belongs to Walther von der Vogelweide), are part of a single song cycle consisting of seventeen songs in five groups: first, songs courting the lady (e.g., MF 215,14; 212,13); second, approach, conflict, separation (206,19; 216,29; and 212,37); third, apostasy and renunciation (207,11; this song is the "middle axis" of the cycle [10]); fourth, hope of winning the lady back, resignation and departure on a Crusade (205,1; 211,27; and 214,12); and fifth, Crusade songs (211,20; 209,25; and 218,5). Despite its employment of state-of-the-art formal criteria, Blattmann's thesis that Hartmann songs were conceived from the beginning as a kind of lyrical novel that documents the vicissitudes of a worldly love and the ultimate rejection of this lower form of love in favor of a higher love for God in the Crusade songs reveals a basically Romantic desire to see the author's lyrical production as a deliberate portrayal of his life events.

Despite continuing attempts to view Hartmann's lyrics as a testimony to events or developments in the life of the poet, many scholars in recent decades have come to view these lyrics as a particular variation within a literary genre that is actually highly conventional and allows little latitude for the expression of private experience. Typical of recent treatments of Hartmann's lyrics, the great variety of which can only be mentioned in this context, is that of Cormeau and Störmer (1985, 81–98), which simply organizes the songs according to five central ideas (complaints, optimistic love songs, women's songs, rejections of *minne* service, and Crusade songs) without attempting to posit their chronology or any personal experiences or development behind them. Many scholars today consider that Hartmann's lyrics can be correctly appraised only by considering the position they occupy within the *Minnesang* corpus as a whole, although the idea that the lyrics are and must be connected to the personal experience of the author continues to be strongly represented. Reusner's 1984 grouping of Hartmann's songs into three groups — songs of high *minne*, songs in which Hartmann distances himself from Chrétien's Laudine figure, and the Crusade songs — concedes that Hartmann's lyrical production is not to be separated from objective instances such as the demands of his patron(s), but nevertheless that they are, on another level, "the expression of (personal) experience" (23). Heinen's 1988 analysis of confession and irony in Hartmann's Song I, MF 205,1, has taken a similar position: "Though scholars — at least in the twentieth century — have stressed the objective quality of medieval literature, some comments in Hartmann's works seem confessional in nature . . ." (417). Jackson's 1994 appraisal takes a middle position on the lyrics, as it does on the narrative works, grouping the love songs objectively into three groups (songs of hope and reciprocal love, complaints at unrewarded service, rejection of love service; 179), but finding aspects particular to Hartmann in the pattern of service and lordship that informed the ministerial knight's social existence (e.g., the attention to the concept of reward) and in the idea that the Crusade lyrics mark a decisive turn away from the tradition of high *minne* (191–93), which implies a development on the part of Hartmann similar to that posited by Wapnewski.

There is as yet no undisputed consensus about where the conventionality of the *Minnesang* language ends and where Hartmann's personal experience begins. It also seems likely, given most of the articles cited here, that scholars will continue trying to identify in the lyrics something more purely personal or subjective pertaining to Hartmann, even as the objective conventionality of the lyrics on a broader level continues to be recognized (although the recent assault on one of the long-standing conventions — the ennobling power of *hohe minne* [cf. Kaplowitt 1986; Willms 1990] — suggests that the objective end of the spectrum is also in flux). There currently seems to be no clear consensus about whether a full recognition of the lyrics' conventionality, on the one hand, and the desire to discover something personal within them, on the other, are mutually exclusive undertakings (there is a conspicuous *in-spite-of-their-conventionality* logic in many of the articles that try to recover something personal) or whether the more strictly objective and more strictly subjective aspects are somehow reconcilable within some broader interpretive framework (Willms [1990] suggests that scholars fell back upon the objective understanding of *Minne* as social ideal that still predominates in literary histories because of an inadequate understanding of *lyric* in terms of *Erlebnisdichtung* [poetry based on personal experience] and that what is necessary is a more adequate definition of *Minnesang* as lyric). For the time being one cannot help but be a bit nostalgic for the simplicity and immediacy of the blood-and-bones conception of Hartmann that scholars such as Schmid and Schreyer possessed, and one is tempted to say that, in the critical history of Hartmann lyrics, increasing knowledge — the placement of Hartmann's lyrics in the framework of broader objective traditions — has led to the rejection of older notions about Hartmann the lyricist without seeming to provide anything unequivocal with which to replace them.

4: *Erec*

Hartmann's *Erec* is considered the first Arthurian romance in Germany that has the court of Arthur and the deeds of its knights as its focal point: "With *Erec* Hartmann introduced Arthurian romance into German literature" (Scherer 1883, 183). The only complete version of this work, which lacks a number of lines from the beginning of the poem, is preserved along with *Die Klage, Iwein,* and works by other authors in the Ambraser Heldenbuch, composed in the early sixteenth century, more than three centuries after the original work. Because of the changes that may have been made to Hartmann's work during this period of time, it seems unlikely, barring the discovery of more manuscripts, that we will ever know the exact constitution of Hartmann's original work. It is useful to bear in mind that Moriz Haupt's (1839) standard edition of this work contains comprehensive emendations and revisions of Ried's text (Schnyder 1987, 313), notably the transformation of Ried's early New High German into a Middle High German idiom that is not necessarily that of Hartmann. Besides the Ambraser manuscript, there are also fragments of destroyed manuscripts in Wolfenbüttel (Herzog August Bibliothek, cod. 19.26.9 Aug.4°) and in Coblenz (Landeshauptarchiv, Best.701 Nr.759,14) from the thirteenth century and in Vienna (Nordösterreichisches Landesarchiv, Nr.821) from the fourteenth century. The scarcity of *Erec* manuscripts suggests that this was not among Hartmann's more popular works in the Middle Ages. Some issues in this work did, however, spark the interest of later poets. Kern (1984) explores direct and implied references to *Erec* in later courtly works such as Wolfram's *Parzival,* Heinrich von dem Türlîn's *Diu Crône,* and *Gauriel von Muntabel,* which indicate a continuing fascination with the *verligen* theme, a critical attitude toward Erec's treatment of Enite, and a certain indecisiveness concerning the question of Enite's guilt, or *Schuld,* which suggests that medieval audiences may have been as puzzled as many modern critics by the apparent necessity of the tribulations she has to undergo.

Hartmann names Chrétien de Troyes as his source in the Wolfenbüttel fragment (als uns Crestiens saget [as Chrétien tells us]; v.4629[12]), but there are many divergences from the text of the French author (many more than in the later *Iwein*). An overemphasis of these divergences led some early German readers to posit Hartmann's complete independence from Chrétien (Barthel 1854, 20). Among the first to devote detailed scrutiny to these divergences was Kleiber (1893), who turned his attention to the relationship of Hartmann's work to that of Chrétien, and to two other versions of the Erec story that were composed at about the same time: the Welsh story "Gereint" of the *Mabinogion* and the Old Norse *Erex* saga. Kleiber notes that many of Hartmann's divergences from Chrétien are also contained in the other versions of the Erec tale, but ultimately he concludes that versions of Chrétien's work served as the source for the other three, in the case of Hartmann's work a lost version (27). Although positing an "absolute dependence" of Hartmann on Chrétien with respect to idea and composition, Kleiber nevertheless considers that Hartmann disposed of the content of the tale in an independent manner, according to his own German, courtly *Gemüt* (character, sensibility) (27). Goedeke's assessment, somewhat more conservative with respect to Hartmann's independence, states that he did not fearfully follow his source (1884, 89). Sparnaay similarly stressed Hartmann's independence, stating that he knew Chrétien, and indeed cites him as a source, but that this citation is of no more value than Wolfram's repeated citation of Kyot as the source of his *Parzival* (Sparnaay believed that Kyot was a real author, whereas most critics today feel that Kyot is an invention and that Chrétien was Wolfram's true source) (1933, 63). The exact relationship of Hartmann to his source(s) has remained an open question, to which many other answers have been put forward. Besides the possibility that a lost version of Chrétien's work served as Hartmann's source, Wapnewski (1962) mentions three other conceivable explanations of Hartmann's divergences from the extant versions of Chrétien's work: 1) the German author relied on his own fantasy, 2) he used other sources besides Chrétien that are also related to the Welsh "Gereint" and the Old Norse *Erex* saga, and 3) he did not base his version on Chrétien's work at all, but rather on a postulated lower Rhenish translation of the work that also served as Chrétien's source (42). Expressing skepticism about Hartmann's use of written sources other than Chrétien and positing yet another possible explanation of discrepancies, the study of Cormeau and Störmer has stated that those divergences of Hartmann from Chrétien which are not based on the former's aesthetic conception are probably based on oral traditions to which Hartmann, as all medieval poets in France and Germany, would have had access (1985, 169).

Striking among the differences between Hartmann's work and that of Chrétien is that the former is significantly longer, containing 10,192 lines as opposed to 6,958 in Chrétien's version (Resler 1987, 20). It is also considered that Hartmann, in contrast to the French author, has a strong proclivity to description and enumeration: portrayals of courtly pageantry, including lists of names he does not seem to have from Chrétien, are more detailed and lengthy with Hartmann. The German author devotes some 500 verses to the description of Enite's saddle where the French author employs only 40; his description of the tournament after Erec's marriage is four times, Enite's lament of Erec's death six times, and the final duel with Mabonagrin three times longer than the corresponding episodes in Chrétien's work. Hartmann diverges from his French predecessor in having Erec depart secretly from Karnant after his fall, in having Erec ask for Enite's forgiveness, in adding the motif of the eighty widows to the joy of the court (*joie de la curt*) adventure, and in the religious tone of the end, which sees Erec return to his homeland, whereas with Chrétien he returns to Arthur's court.

These and many other differences between Hartmann and Chrétien were once explained with reference to what were seen as attributes of national character: the French author was viewed as realistic, rational, and carefree, while the German was seen as idealistic, profound, and loyal (for discussion of this tendency see Wapnewski 1962, 43, and Trimborn 1985, 10–19). Typical in this respect is the contrast made by Kleiber between the German author's greater depth of thought and feeling and the French author's more shallow approach (1893, 21), between Hartmann's ability to fill his portrayal with an exact and sensitive knowledge of the human heart and Chrétien's lack of warm sensitivity and of depth of thought (29). Clichés with respect to national character, such as Jantzen's view that the German works are distinguished from the French sources in their glorification of loyalty and manly courage (1933, 8), have gradually given way to a less ideologically laden consideration of the differing political and social constellations in which the two authors worked. A widely held view today is that the German author is more courtly than his French source, that he reveals a marked tendency to smooth out rough edges and to diminish or eliminate material contained in Chrétien that is seen to be more course and garish (Wiehl 1974, 191): this toning down of the more colorful and loud French original for a different audience in Germany corresponds to what French Hartmann scholars have called the "adaptation courtoise" (Huby 1974 and Fourquet 1977). Hartmann is also typically seen to be more pedagogical in his approach to his material than Chrétien (Resler 1987, 20). Despite some objections on methodological grounds (Voß argues that the attempt to identify what is Hartmann's inevitably applies a standard of originality that is foreign to the Middle Ages; 1983, 177–78) and general recognition of Hartmann's strong allegiance to Chrétien, it is also thought that Hartmann's divergences from Chrétien can be grasped by the modern critic in terms of a coherent and independent artistic conception on the part of the German author. The fact that Hartmann stays so close to Chrétien much of the time is itself taken as an indication that the critic needs to pay close attention to those instances where he diverges from him (Linke 1968, 155). Keller, in the foreword of his 1987 English translation of *Erec,* gives voice to this prevalent tendency: "Any deviations from the original text must be considered to be intentional" (xv). According to Cormeau and Störmer, the effect of Hartmann's divergences from Chrétien is to focus more closely on the development of the figure of Erec; correspondingly, Enite's activity is somewhat reduced: she becomes the image of constancy and suffering perfection (1985, 173).

Early scholarly appraisals were frequently negative. Gervinus, directing his criticism at both *Erec* and *Iwein,* states that a greater depth of insight is missing from these two poems, which lack formal coherence and portray and recount much which is incomprehensible (1853, 369). Barthel writes: "With respect to the poetic value of the poem, it is most regrettable that Hartmann came across this barren Welsh material (1854, 32). Pfeiffer considers *Erec* "not exactly a masterpiece," and not nearly as good as *Iwein* (1859, 8). Looking for coherent development in the seemingly random adventures and for individual depth in characterizations that seemed all too schematic, these early scholarly assessments failed to perceive any broader artistic conception or structure in *Erec.* Barthel speaks of a "Don Quixote-like search for adventures, which hang together only very loosely" (1854, 32). Kleiber recognizes a unity of conception, although he also considers that *Erec* consists of somewhat randomly arranged adventures, which "in their loose connection have been put in not only to develop the idea, but also for their own sake" (1893, 28). Sparnaay also perceived no broader conceptual unity in this work. Despite recognizing "an inner transformation of the hero," Sparnaay voiced skepticism about whether the various single episodes form "a coherent, original work" (1933, 67).

Rather than interpreting Hartmann's *Erec* on its own terms, Sparnaay turned his attention to this work's connections to Celtic myth, which enabled him to establish insightful connections between the romances of Chrétien and Hartmann, on the one hand, and mythical themes and motifs on the other. The name of Gereint, for example, for which Erec was probably a later substitution, might be traced back to an early-eighth-century British king named Geruntius (63–64). On the Continent Gereint was changed to Weroc, possibly the hero of a orally transmitted tale involving a hunt for a stag (72), and this name eventually evolved into Erec. The name of Enite is based on the earlier Celtic form Enid [forest lark] (72). The presence of many versions of the tales upon which *Erec* was based, according to Sparnaay, is attested to by the presence of a version of the story of the contest for the sparrow hawk in Andreas Capellanus's treatise *De amore* (On

Love) (70). Sparnaay's approach to Hartmann's *Erec* views it primarily as a kind of repository of its presumed mythical sources. The adventures of Erec following the Karnant episode, Sparnaay argues, have a double motivation: the demonstration of Erec's heroic qualities as a response to his erotic lapse at Karnant and the testing of Enite's marital fidelity. These two mythical themes, according to Sparnaay, have only recently been combined, and the connection of both to Celtic myth is seen as contrary to the idea of a creative author with a coherent conception or program (101–2). Thus, the problem of Chrétien's influence over Hartmann has been to some extent pushed aside in favor of a view that posits the influence of mythical materials over both.

The connection to Celtic myth may not assist scholars much in arriving at an interpretation of the works on their own merits, but it does point to an ongoing difficulty in interpreting works such as *Erec*: the mythical lore may have continued to possess its own compelling logic, which would have set limitations to the extent to which the poets such as Chrétien and Hartmann could alter it (cf. also the discussion of mythical elements in *Iwein*). In some cases, such as Erec's cruel treatment of Enite, the Arthurian works seem to combine older mythical motifs (the test of the unfaithful wife) with other concerns of a social, ethical, and/or political kind. Since the logic of these different themes, motifs, and concerns goes in different directions, this makes the interpretation of such episodes difficult. The connections of Arthurian romance to Celtic myth is taken up in the study of Ó Riain-Raedel (1978).

The early tendency to focus on isolated aspects of *Erec* and on their presumed sources without recognizing any higher unifying principle has given way to the recognition that this work is a tightly organized narrative that contains the prototypical, or "classical," structure of Arthurian romance first devised by Chrétien de Troyes and continued in Germany by Hartmann von Aue and Wolfram von Eschenbach. Kuhn's influential *Erec* essay differs from earlier studies, which may have left their readers with the mistaken impression that *Erec* is a *Machwerk* [a concoction, bungling work] (1948, 41) by drawing attention to this structural design, which organizes the seemingly random series of adventures that make up the plot of the Arthurian works into a bipartite structure. Each structural segment involves the hero's departure from court (generally the court of Arthur), a series of adventures, and the hero's return to court. Meaning is to be sought not so much in the thematic content of these two structural segments as in their relationship to one another. Although the first segment sees Erec win a wife and land, along with the status conferred upon him by the court of Arthur, his achievements are not substantial until the second series of adventures has occurred, which follows a crisis that appears to place everything the knight has previously done in question. The meaning of the relationship of the two structural segments is linked to a religious form of thinking in the manner of a structural analogy: the crisis following the first segment and initiating the second is analogous to man's fall from grace. It implies that the hero cannot extricate himself from sin/guilt (*Schuld*) and achieve true happiness by his own strength and of his own volition, despite his best intentions. In this respect the hero is representative of the human condition as viewed in the Middle Ages. His sin/guilt is not of a personal or subjective nature, as it might be understood today, but rather objective or trans-personal: it rests in the very constitution of human flesh and the unredeemed world. The second series of adventures does not so much respond to the first as transcend it, by bringing the hero to a spiritually more enlightened condition in which his achievements are recognized as originating not in his own abilities but in God. The structural coherence provided by the relationship of the two narrative segments to one another is further reinforced by Kuhn's recognition that the series of adventures themselves are not random, but rather tightly organized in systems of correspondences, so that the significance of each episode can be viewed not only with respect to its own thematic content, but also in its relationship to the earlier or later adventures to which it corresponds (e.g., there are two adventures with counts; two battles with Guivreiz). (It should be mentioned here that in the structure pointed out by Kuhn, the final adventure of *joie de la curt* occurs after the conclusion of the second segment of adventures. The structural prominence of this adventure corresponds to its status as a commentary on the whole story: Kuhn considers that this strict isolation of Mabonagrin and his wife from courtly society alludes to the earlier erotic lapse of Erec and Enite, which also isolated them from the court. The majority of scholars have concurred in agreeing that the *joie de la curt* episode is to be read in some way or another as a succinct commentary on Erec and Enite's own development.)

Kuhn's insights opened up new possibilities of interpretation by grounding *Erec* (and the other Arthurian works that follow the same pattern) at the structural level in currents of medieval religious thought. It seemed to become feasible to find in structure the deeper meaning that early readers and critics such as Barthel had considered to be absent at the level of plot. Kuhn's *Erec* essay thus rejected what had been one of the foundations of previous Hartmann criticism, which was that the knightly adventures could be viewed in terms of a modern, linear kind of individual development (however poorly such development seemed to be realized), replacing this with a specifically medieval form of "development" that is discontinuous from a modern perspective. It is notable that Kuhn elsewhere takes positions that seem less consistently objective, for example when he defines the adventure as *autonome Selbstentwicklung* [autonomous development of self] (1959b, 35).

Two more recent (1987) conceptions of the work's structure are those of Resler and Keller. In commentaries accompanying their English translations of *Erec,* they have posited different but equally valid conceptions of the work's structure that reveal its tight organization. *Erec,* just as all of Chrétien's works, Hartmann's *Iwein,* and Wolfram von Eschenbach's *Parzival,* can be divided according to Resler (22–24) into five distinct segments: first, the exposition, beginning at the court of King Arthur, in which an incident requires the hero to leave the court (Erec's insult by the dwarf of Iders); second, a first series of adventures that culminates in the hero's apparent happiness (Erec's victory over Iders, his fame at the tournament at Arthur's court, and his marriage to Enite); third, a catastrophe for the hero in which he is accused of some error (Erec ignores his knightly responsibilities and overhears Enite lamenting the shame he has brought upon them); fourth, a second series of adventures that functions as an atonement (the series of adventures culminating in that of *joie de la curt)*; and fifth, the conclusion, in which the hero attains a condition of true happiness (Erec, reunited with his wife, rejoins the court of Arthur with high honor and later returns to his native land Destrigales). The advantage enjoyed by a model such as this over the more conventional bipartite structure, although the two conceptions are by no means mutually exclusive, is that it devotes more detailed attention to the moments (i.e., the first, third, and fifth segments) preceding and following each of the two series of adventures (the second and fourth segments). In so doing, it begins to move away from the idea of the bipartite structure as reflective of an essentially religious form of thinking toward a more thematically oriented conception of structure based on the predictable occurrence of certain kinds of episodes from work to work. Positing a structure that is somewhat closer to the bipartite structure of Kuhn, but also more thematic in its orientation, Keller (xxiii) posits numerous correspondences between the first structural segment and the last (Roman numerals denote the structural segments, Arabic numerals the episodes that correspond to one another): I. 1. Erec's failure, 2. the Iders plot (Erec and Enite appear together), 3. Return to Arthur, 4. Test at Arthur's court (Erec and Enite are separated for the tournament), 5. Fight with Roiderodes at the tournament (Erec and Enite embody the ideals of *minne* and knighthood); II. 1. Erec's transgression (*verligen*), 2. First series of adventures (Erec and Enite are together), 3. Return to Arthur's court, 4. Second series of adventure, from that involving Cardoc to the second battle with Guivreiz (Erec and Enite are completely separated from each other), 5. *Joie de la curt* (Erec and Enite embody the ideal of the marital relationship). Unlikely to gain wide acceptance, but indicative of the variety of frames of reference brought to bear in appraisals of this work, is the "eccentric philological experiment" of Katzenmeier (1989, 8), who puts forward the thesis that Hartmann's *Erec* is structured analogously to medieval chess. The action of the work amounts to an allegory of a chess game, in which the white figures stand for the hero's friends and the black for his enemies (since Enite is equivalent to the white queen, and white symbolizes purity, Katzenmeier concludes that Enite is "completely free of guilt" [23]).

Interpretation of the work has revolved around the Karnant episode: a knight who has established a reputation for himself temporarily loses himself in the carnal pleasures of the newlywed and forgets about the deeds upon which knightly fame is based. Upon discovering the disregard into which he has fallen, he sets out to correct his error in the renewed pursuit of knightly combat. It is more or less in this way that critics such as Barthel and Kleiber saw the work. Closer scrutiny of this work has in the last few decades yielded what has been called "a bewildering variety of interpretations" (Ranawake 1988, 93) that qualify this basic appraisal in many ways. Most significant for the history of the critical reception of *Erec* and still dominant in recent interpretations is the idea of individual development. Seen in such terms, Erec's sudden lapse at Karnant, his *verligen,* is not itself the problem, but rather the symptom of a deeper problem/weakness that was already in Erec previous to the Karnant episode and that is in some way solved/overcome in the adventures of the second structural segment. The developmental interpretations might be divided into the more purely religious/spiritual and the more purely ethical/secular, although a dividing line between these two concerns is often difficult to draw, as a sample of some of the more recent interpretations indicates.

An overtly religious interpretation of Erec's adventures is that of Tax, who posits that the work is structured like a triptych: the first section describes Erec's path as a young knight that culminates in marriage, the second (ending in Erec's Lazarus-like resurrection in the Oringles episode) solidifies Erec's marital relationship to Enite, and the third brings Erec to the highest form of knighthood based on the Christian virtue of *caritas* (charity), which takes him beyond his previous concupiscence and his resulting "prideful self-isolation" (1963, 291). Recently Fisher has continued the religious line of interpretation, positing that Erec's basic problem is one of the seven deadly sins: *superbia* (pride). Hartmann, in a much more consistent manner than Chrétien, employs the motifs of voice and speech prohibition in order to demonstrate how Erec gradually learns to repress "his own masculine individuality." Erec does this by listening to the voice of "reason," which is that of his wife, Enite, who is viewed by Fisher as the embodiment of humility (1986, 371). The Cadoc episode marks the beginning of this positive transformation in Erec, for it is here that he reacts for the first time positively to the voice of a woman. Although not insisting on a strictly religious interpretation of the work, Tobler has pointed out that Erec sometimes manifests features of a Christian redeemer figure (1986, 427) and that Enite is correspondingly described with many of the same images that are used in the Bible, sermons, and mystical literature to describe the Virgin Mary, such as the images of the lily (verse 337) and the moon (verse 1766–81) that are employed to portray Enite's great beauty (432). Consistent with such descriptions, according to Tobler, is the idea that the relationship between Erec and Enite becomes spiritually deepened to the point that Enite might be regarded as analogous to the "mystical bride" of medieval mystical literature. In the case of the final *joie de la curt* episode, their mystical togetherness means that physical proximity is no longer necessary for the lovers to draw strength from one another (438). For Ranawake, Erec's *verligen* stems from another of the seven deadly sins: sloth. Ranawake points out that Hartmann dwells to a lesser extent than Chrétien on describing the marital pleasures that lead other critics to condemn Erec for concupiscence, and she posits that Hartmann has instead chosen to focus on the hero's sloth: "Erec, it appears, has contrived a way to reduce his professional, social, and religious obligations to an absolute minimum" (1988, 97). In order to highlight the hero's pervasive sloth, Hartmann has, according to Ranawake, taken pains to portray Erec as the opposite of a sluggard before and after his fall at Karnant (103). Sloth represents only a temporarily failing that is overcome by Erec, who emerges in the *joie de la curt* episode as "the anti-type not only of the slothful knight, but of slothful man as such, an exemplary soldier of Christ" (109). The article of Jacobson, one of many studies focusing on the problem of language, posits that a "lack of vigilance" on the part of Erec allows a gulf to open up between word and meaning (1991, 124); Erec's fall thus constitutes a descent into linguistic chaos, symbolic of a diabolical subversion of the divine coincidence of the word with its meaning (125). Erec's defeat of Kay, who for Jacobson is the embodiment of the divergence of word and meaning, marks the point at which Erec begins to establish a "monophonic language" in which word and significance correspond.

Articles positing problems of a less overtly religious kind have also focused on a broad spectrum of possible flaws and transgressions. Cramer (1972) regards Erec's problem as a social one: by marrying Enite, Erec has inappropriately ignored the social distance that separates them. This distance is overcome in the second series of adventures, in which Erec and Enite come to recognize each other as social equals. Kalinke sees Erec's fault in his inability to recognize that fame, after it has been achieved, has to be constantly reaffirmed (1976, 74).

The article of McConeghy (1987) examines the problem of women's speech from a cultural standpoint, particularly the strategies that Enite employs to communicate vital information to Erec, despite his prohibition of speech, and to avoid the punishment he has threatened (i.e., death). Enite's words indicate especially the employment of negative-politeness strategies, typical in strongly patriarchal societies, to diminish the impact of her speech upon Erec. McConeghy nevertheless feels that Hartmann advocates a more active and vocal role for women in the marriage relationship than is visible on the surface. Firestone (1988), departing from the thesis that Hartmann's work is simultaneously secular and religious in nature, sees in it a conception of the relationship of order and disorder that is analogous to moral-theological ideas in Boethius's *Consolatio Philosophiae*. The basic flaw of Erec and Enite is that they do not recognize that happiness is one and simple in nature, but rather seek it in its separate parts (120). This results among other things in Erec's recklessness in his initial adventures: he "abandons" the queen and her servant after the dwarf's insult, and he "rashly" promises to marry Enite in order to achieve the arms he needs to fight Iders (119). Both at the tournament at Arthur's court and at Karnant the behavior of Erec, and of Enite as well, is "immoderate and inconsistent" (120). This flawed orientation is overcome in the second series of adventures, in which Erec and Enite act without conflicting emotion in the service of others, simultaneously demonstrating the place of their marriage in the divine order (121). Clark's study (1989) posits that *Erec* focuses on the mechanics of how thought is transformed into action. Focusing on the problem of speech in a manner that is, in some respects, similar to the studies of Fisher and Jacobson, Clark argues that Erec's adventures reflect a process in which he moves from an initially high degree of verbal ability in the Tulmein episode, to a period following his troubles at Karnant when he not only lapses into silence, but also imposes silence upon others, to a final condition in which Erec has recovered the ability to "frame words — and structure situations — to his benefit" (63). See returns to the idea of recklessness, positing that it is not just a symptom but Erec's central problem: Erec "concentrates all his energies, or focuses all his attention, on one thing at a time, to the exclusion and detriment of everything else" (1991, 39). Like Firestone, See considers many of Erec's actions in the first sequence of adventures (e.g., his offer to marry Enite in exchange for arms) to be rash and inappropriate (41). Erec is also, for See, too obsessed with the idea of winning, as is indicated by his behavior at the tournament at Arthur's court, which Erec takes far more seriously than the other knights. In the second series of adventures Erec faces "educative challenges" which bring him to protect Enite rather than to punish her, to see the misery of other people, and to recognize "the value of real contact with people" (52). Quast posits, in a manner that is reminiscent of Ruh's approach to *Erec* (1993, 1967), that the establishment of the proper kind of marriage is the central issue in this work. Quast contributes the idea that an insufficient conception of marriage based on feudal practice, dynastic considerations, and the production of heritable offspring in the conjugal bed (represented by Erec's *verligen* at Karnant) is replaced by a *literary* conception of marriage that combines feudal elements with literary elements from the courtly love tradition. The result of this combination is a freely adopted relationship of reciprocity between man and woman based on *triuwe* (fidelity, loyalty). The development of Erec and Enite is for Quast a question of arriving at this kind of reciprocal marriage relationship.

The 1994 book of Jackson, which assesses all of Hartmann's works in their relationship to twelfth-century chivalry in Germany and views Hartmann as a representative of the lower ministerial class and as a link between clerical and chivalric cultures, takes into consideration those studies (cf. Voß, Fischer; discussed below) which are critical of the idea of individual development, stating that past interpretations have been too vaguely idealizing and unhistorical and conceding that the romances of Hartmann (as those of Chrétien) contain an element of deep-rooted, self-assertive violence (136). Jackson's study may be cited here because it considers that these studies, despite their merit, underplay "the ethical dynamism and the emotional finesse of Hartmann's treatment of knighthood in the figure of the main protagonist" (137). Development in the sense of an increasing moral reflection is present in *Erec*, according to Jackson, even if the value of violent force for the knightly class (i.e., the ministerials and the free nobles, who are bound together by the knightly ideology despite their legal differences) is not being renounced but only channelled and contained, in a manner that reflects the attempt of German peace laws in the last third of the twelfth century to steer and limit warfare (139). In *Erec,* these different elements are combined in what Jackson calls an "ethics of force."

Influential in interpretations based on individual development has been the idea that Erec begins the work as a tabula rasa, receiving the appropriate formation only after the many adventures that he has yet to undertake. Kuhn remarks that Erec in the company of the queen at the beginning of the work is "in a neutral situation" since he is involved neither in courtly representation (i.e., the hunt for the white stag) nor in adventures (1948, 41). More recently, Clark has called Erec during the same part of the work "a clean slate" (1989, 54). Another frequent assumption is that the court of King Arthur that figures so prominently in this work can be used as a kind of measuring device with which the progress of the hero can be assessed: "Clearly, the Arthurian court (symbolized by the Round Table) provides the most visible yardstick for measuring the hero's acceptance or rejection by society" (Resler 1987, 23). Some scholars posit that the development that transforms the hero from his tabula rasa condition into the completely formed figure as which he presents himself at the end of his adventures takes him even beyond the values represented by the court of King Arthur. This tendency, which is far more pronounced in scholarship dealing with Hartmann's later work *Iwein,* is exemplified by Kuhn, who states that *Erec* does not serve the idealization of courtly values, but rather their criticism (1953), by Tax, who feels that the development of spiritual qualities transcends and implicitly criticizes knightly values (1963), and more recently by Thomas, who also posits that Erec's spiritual development takes him to a condition that transcends the worldly values of Arthurian knighthood: "The basically secular nature of the Arthurian ethic made it incompatible with medieval Christianity . . . . The ideal society was not Arthur's, but that headed at the end by the humble and God-fearing King Erec" (1982, 18).

Despite views such as these, many scholars consider that *Erec,* in contrast to the later narrative works, does not move beyond a reaffirmation of worldly Arthurian values. Eroms's study (1970) undertakes to demonstrate that the word *vreude* (joy) is used in a purely secular sense, implying that a basically spiritual term has been replaced in this work by an immanent, worldly one, and Schröder's study concurs that courtly joy (i.e., the values of Arthur's court) are not placed in question (1972, 310). Steinle, who focuses her attention on the language used to refer to individuals, states that this language, in the specific case of Erec, allows for no conclusions about his presumed guilt, for he is neither criticized nor condemned (1978, 82). Notable in this context is Voß's thesis that the idea of Erec's developing beyond the values of Arthur's court is sometimes rejected with the covert motive of viewing this work as the imperfect anticipation of the later *Iwein* (in which such growth is more generally postulated) (1983, 84); thus, the idea of development is not so much given up as transferred to Hartmann's literary career. Voß, as will be seen below, dismisses the idea of a development of the hero beyond Arthur in *both* the Arthurian works as an anachronistic search for individuality.

Although the figure of Erec is subjected to the greatest amount of scrutiny, critics have also considered that Enite undergoes a developmental process in which a flaw or guilt is overcome. Despite difficulties in pinpointing any specific transgression on her part, some have argued that Enite accrues guilt for Erec's fall at Karnant. It has been suggested, for instance, that Enite is guilty for not telling her husband openly of the shame into which he has fallen (most recently by McConeghy 1987, 780; Sterba 1991, 59–60). However, the proposition that Enite is to blame for the ruin of Erec's reputation remains hotly contested among scholars. Kuhn, in his *Erec* essay (1948), calls her one of the purest women figures of the Middle Ages and modernity, denying even the possibility of *Mitschuld* [guilt by association] (48), although in another essay he posits precisely such a *Mitschuld* (1953, 77). Ruh (1967, 112–14), and subsequently Smits (1981) and Quast (1993; discussed above), avoid to some extent the problem of Enite's possible guilt by positing that the central problem of the work is arriving at the right kind of marriage; the problem is thus not so much in Erec or in Enite individually, as in their relationship to each other, which the hardships endured by both — although they are of a different nature — are seen to solidify. Smits stresses the religious character of the marriage, which she sees as consistent with patristic and early Scholastic discussions of marriage as a relationship in which both partners are able to develop their potential fully (24). Despite the difficulty of locating a specific transgression to which her later trials and tribulations might be meaningfully connected, one has to bear in mind, as Voß points out (1983, 94), that Enite is viewed as the cause of Erec's neglect of knightly responsibilities by the inhabitants of Karnant and that she explicitly accepts this judgment as her own. On the other hand, women figures in the works of Hartmann, as has been pointed out in the 1970 study of women figures by Carne, frequently embody values and abilities (Carne names goodness [*güete*], practical realism, communication, healing, and compassion as characteristic of female characters) that the heroes have to achieve in the efforts of their adventures (147). According to a view such as this, Erec's harsh treatment should not be seen as indicative of a shortcoming on Enite's part, but rather as an ongoing demonstration of a failing within the hero himself which he is in the process of overcoming. Erec ends, according to this view, by acquiring some quality, such as goodness or compassion, that Enite has had from the start.

A few recent studies have questioned whether it is appropriate at all to apply the category of individual development to this work. The study of Voß is based on the thesis that the idea of objectivity as defined in Kuhn's *Erec* essay is not compatible with the notion of individual development and that the latter notion inevitably projects modern aesthetic categories (that of the *Bildungsroman*) onto the medieval works: "Nicht das Individuum ist also die Bezugsgröße in diesem fiktiven System, sondern ein überindividuelles ideales Ganzes, als dessen Teil sich der Einzelne begreift und zur Geltung bringt" [The individual is not the frame of reference in this fictive system, but rather a transpersonal ideal totality of which the individual considers himself a part and brings to bear] (1983, 14). Attempting to apply the typological structure pointed out by Kuhn in a more consistently objective manner, Voß stresses the perfection of the hero at the outset of the work, rather than the unformed, neutral condition that is posited elsewhere. This perfection insures that Erec does not undergo anything resembling development in the modern sense and that positing flaws of an ethical nature inappropriately projects such a conception of development onto works that do not contain it. The fall of Erec is objective in the strict sense of the word: it is not linked to any *specific* individual problem that could be identified in the first series of adventures, in which the hero corresponds perfectly to feudal-aristocratic ideals. Erec's fall at Karnant is not linked to any internal deficiency; he falls from his high position according to the logic of a transpersonal, Augustinian conception of guilt, according to which all humans, even the most exemplary, are linked to the sins of their ancestors (74–80). The second series of adventures is a secularized form of penance that restores the hero to his original state of perfection.

According to the psychoanalytically oriented study of Steiner (1983), Erec's journeys through the work can be seen as development or progress only within the context of the patriarchal court society, whose male values and interests they reaffirm. Within the context of a broader cultural model, in which rational, "enlightened" patriarchal social orders (e.g., the knightly order of Hartmann, the bourgeois order of Sigmund Freud) are achieved by means of the ongoing repression of an original matriarchal existence (for which *libido* is one of the associated terms), Erec's journeys are seen by Steiner as a form of regression that confronts the mythic remnants of this other feminine existence in the name of a "an aristocratic community of male comradeship" (11). The adventure thus involves the suppression of the sexuality embodied initially by Enite (13) and, on another level, the imposition of courtly order on the dangerous mythical (matriarchal) wilds surrounding Arthur's court (26–37). Hartmann's undertaking is thus similar to that of Freud in its broader cultural function, except that the matriarchal remnants still presented themselves to the medieval author as an alternative existence that had to be made taboo, whereas these remnants presented themselves to Freud in terms of pathology (7).

Czerwinski's book on German court literature (1989), which contains a chapter on *Erec,* attempts to refine the approach taken in Fischer's 1983 study of *Iwein* and is based on the assumption that forms of reflection and abstraction among lay nobility in the High Middle Ages were very rudimentary and inseparable from visibility and materiality. Identity does not yet organize different realms of experience hierarchically — as it does in modern times — into what is on the surface (i.e., the ego) and what is concealed beneath (the unconscious), but rather as an aggregate, in which social forms that appear contradictory to the modern eye (e.g., the abstract mediation of courtliness versus unmediated feudal aggression) continue to exist visibly side by side. Based on this assumption, Czerwinski argues that

Erec's honor and the injury to it are made possible by a split in consciousness characteristic of this earliest phase of self-reflection: there is another realm in which the peaceful courtly forms of the Arthurian court have no validity. Inverting the thesis that Erec acts rashly in pursuing Iders, Czerwinski argues that this pursuit takes the place of an immediate attack that would result in the unarmed Erec's death and is, consequently, demonstrative of reflection and restraint. In the contest for the sparrow hawk, a split in consciousness indicative of reflection is introduced by the suggestion that Erec would win even if Enite were blacker than coal (verse 653); this however gives way to the typically medieval coincidence of nobility, beauty, and strength that is established in Erec's victory. Erec's *verligen* is seen not as an individual failing, but rather as the loss of the possibility of courtly abstraction (on a broader historical level this possibility is linked to a reorganization of power [*Gewalt*] at the territorial level). Such mediation now being absent, Erec himself reverts in the subsequent adventures to unreflected forms of violence characteristic of the feudal lord in his relations both to his wife and to military opponents. In the *joie de la curt* adventure courtly mediation is reconstituted, paradoxically by means of the greatest exercise of violence. At the moment of its greatest intensity, violence is replaced *sprunghaft* (by means of a jump) by the pacific forms of courtliness. Noteworthy is Czerwinski's criticism of past critical approaches that are based on an unproblematical and unhistorical conception of individual identity, intentionality, and moral reflection. For Czerwinski, the identity taken for granted by many modern critics does not yet exist in the medieval works.

Another recent example of a shift from individual development to a more strictly objective, or transpersonal, critical frame of reference is provided by the article of Ehrismann (1989). Addressing what he calls the "Individualitätspriorität" [priority of individuality] in scholarship dealing with the Arthurian works, Ehrismann posits that it is incumbent on advocates of the idea of individual development to demonstrate the poet's positive interest in the formation of individual identity, as well as a consistently articulated transformation on the part of the hero that overtly corresponds to this interest. In his own analysis of Hartmann's *Erec*, Ehrismann argues that these two requisites are not present: decisive plot actions are weakly or ambivalently motivated, if they are motivated at all (e.g., Erec's decision at Karnant to embark on adventures, his command of silence to Enite). Rather than individual development, Ehrismann observes in this particular work a variety of elements that are representative of various aspects of courtly life.

The studies of Voß, Steiner, Czerwinski, and Ehrismann criticize in different ways the idea of individual development that is the central assumption of the vast majority of Erec interpretations. They do so by focusing on the hero's initial condition, not as a clean slate to which something has to be added in some sort of process of self-improvement, but rather as socially and culturally conditioned in some way or another from the outset. Stress is therefore placed on the initial orientation and on how the hero's adventures impose this orientation on the world and not on the way in which the initial orientation is given up in favor of some superior one in a developmental process. In these studies the primary question is not so much how the world makes a mark on Erec, perfecting his initially insufficient and/or immature internal condition, but rather how he imposes his own order on the world, giving it an imprint that is not only his own, but also — for better or worse — that of the feudal aristocratic community to which he belongs.

5: *Gregorius*

SIX COMPLETE MANUSCRIPTS and five fragments of *Gregorius* are preserved from the thirteenth to the fifteenth century. Wapnewski characterizes the transmission of this work as "not good, but at least better than *Erec* and *Der arme Heinrich*" (1962, 76). The prologue is preserved in only two of the manuscripts (designated *J* [Staatsbibliothek Stiftung Preußischer Kulturbesitz, Berlin; Ms. germ. qu. 979] and *K* [Stadtarchiv, Konstanz; Hs. A I 1]). Some have believed it possible that the prologue was not a part of the original work, but rather a later addition by another author (Sparnaay 1933, 73), but most consider it Hartmann's own composition (Wolf 1964, 8). The oldest preserved version of the Gregorius story — and the immediate source of Hartmann's work — is the French *Vie du Pape Grégoire*, which was likely composed around the middle of the twelfth century at the court of Henry II and Eleanor of Aquitaine (Mertens 1978a, 27). Possibly significant with respect to the audience for which Hartmann's work was composed is Mertens's statement that this French source is thinkable only in the milieu of lay nobility, since the titular hero was not an official saint (22). This strongly suggests that Hartmann's work was also composed for a lay noble audience, which, in fact, is the general assumption among scholars, whatever their position may be with respect to the work's religiosity. Whether one of the six preserved versions of the French *Grégoire* served as Hartmann's source, or whether he based his work on a lost manuscript of this work is, according to Wapnewski, a matter of debate (1962, 81). Sparnaay mentions many other medieval versions of the Gregorius story besides the manuscripts of *Grégoire*: a shorter French version of the story from the last years of the fourteenth century, three manuscripts of an English poem, a prose version that was included in a collection of saints' lives, a so-called *Volksbuch* [chapbook], and four Latin versions of the story (including that of the *Gesta Romanorum*) (1933, 127–28). Hartmann's treatment of his French source has been analyzed in detail by Schottmann (1965), who observed the tendency — visible also in Hartmann's treatment of his other sources — to make more abstract and normative a source that was more dependent on impulsiveness and immediacy of characterization and motivation (397). The study of Herlem-Prey (1979), a detailed comparison of the French *Grégoire* manuscripts with one another and with the work of Hartmann, also finds an "adaptation courtoise" in the German work and posits that Hartmann's work is not based on any of the preserved French versions of the work, but rather on a common archetype. The fifteenth-century New High German prose version of Hartmann's work contained in the saints' lives (Innsbruck UB Cod.631) has been recently edited by Plate (1983); the literary reception of the tale of Gregorius in Germany subsequent to Hartmann is discussed by Mertens (1978a, 105–52).

Critics have long stressed the similarities of this tale to the Greek tragedy of Sophocles: "Gregorius is a medieval Oedipus" (Scherer 1883, 181). In fact, Hartmann's *Gregorius* is one of many tales, myths, and legends in the Middle Ages that revolve around the theme of incest. It is not known upon whom the story is based: the protagonist cannot be identified with any of the historical popes by the name of Gregorius (Wapnewski 1962, 80). Citing Freud, Sparnaay points out the omnipresence of the theme of incest in mythology and literature around the world, notable examples being Zeus and Hera, Isis and Osiris, Lot and his daughters (1933, 149). The universality of this theme prevents direct connections from being established between the Greek tragedy and Hartmann's work. Nevertheless, Sparnaay is struck by similarities in detail shared by the Gregorius story as composed by Hartmann and a Persian story in the Firdûsîs Book of Kings concerning a hero named Dârâb that was written in the first decades of the eleventh century. Both tales contain the giving of valuables to the abandoned child, the use of these riches to educate the child, the fight with playmates, the lack of desire to follow in the footprints of the adopted father, the love for warfare, the quarrel with the adopted mother, who finally reveals his false identity (155).

A significant article dealing specifically with *Gregorius* and the tragedy of Sophocles is that of Zuntz (1954), who sets out to establish some of the significant differences between the classical and the medieval work. Most important, according to Zuntz, is the lack of pathos in the medieval tale. The unlimited and hopeless suffering of the Greek hero has been replaced in the Gregorius story by a suffering that contains the greatest meaning, because it is connected to the Christian ideas of sinfulness and penance. While the Greek hero struggles without hope between the order of the *polis* and chaos, the suffering of the Christian hero, who, reaching the limits of his own abilities and faculties, submits himself to the will of God is an act of penance with high spiritual significance (105–7). Notable about Zuntz's evaluation of *Gregorius* is that he does not view it in terms of the theological literature of Hartmann's day, nor does he find a specific individual guilt or sin on the part of Gregorius, whose is merely a representative figure. Both of these positions are exceptional, given the predominantly theological orientation and the search for sin that elsewhere dominated *Gregorius* interpretation until the sixties.

The recent article of Buschinger (1985) discusses the motif of incest in medieval literature on a broader level and focuses more specifically on its legal ramifications. Although incest is punished in the Bible and was punishable by death according to some Germanic legal codices, Buschinger states that incest is hardly ever mentioned in medieval law. There are even indications that it was viewed as a sexual deviation among many others (135). Interestingly, it was in poetic texts such as *Gregorius* that incest was considered a great sin (135). Buschinger also concludes that incest was seldom viewed as a sign of being chosen by God (136); this conclusion implicitly conflicts with many interpretations that view Gregorius as a spiritually exemplary figure. Consistent with most interpretations is the gap pointed out by Buschinger between the theological conception, in which incest did not receive much attention, and the popular conception (visible in literary works such as Hartmann's), in which incest appears as the profoundest of sins. The legal implications of incest is also a focal point of Cormeau and Störmer, who point out that the child of an incestuous relationship is "a social non-person," excluded from inheritance and social position (1985, 120–21).

The prologue has drawn an inordinate amount of critical attention, not only because it is preserved in only two of the manuscripts (its authorship by Hartmann has been questioned by some scholars, such as Sparnaay 1933, 73), but also because of its unusual length (Pretzel 1979 posits fifty-one verses) and because the author here seems to present himself to us in an uncharacteristically direct and emotional way. Machule anticipates one of the major assumptions of later theologically oriented interpretations by arguing that the prologue, which is based on and demonstrates a close familiarity with the language of the Bible and theological literature, prepares the reader to receive the message of the work (1900, 211). The essay of Bennholdt-Thomsen (1962) focuses on one part of the prologue — the clothes (*kleit*), symbolizing fear (*vorhte*) and hope (*gedingen*) that God gives to the man who has fallen among robbers — in order to cover himself. Hartmann's insertion of these symbolic clothes, which are subsequently linked to the idea of penance, is for Bennholdt-Thomsen based on the parable of the lost son, elements of which have been added to the more obvious biblical model which is the parable of the good Samaritan. Bennholdt-Thomsen argues that this does not indicate confusion on the part of Hartmann with respect to the Bible (he had been accused of such by Schönbach 1894, 130, and Wapnewski speaks of "a confused rendition of the parable of the Good Samaritan," 1962, 77). Rather, Hartmann's combination of the two parables allows him, in anticipation of his own subject matter, to combine the motifs of divine clemency and penance, and this combination is consistent with patristic exegesis; indeed, Hartmann closely follows the exegesis of Bede (202–7). More recently, the importance of Bede, and the employment of the parable of the lost son, has been placed in doubt (Mertens 1978a, 170–71). Wapnewski (1962) finds the prologue *auffallend* [conspicuous] in the context of all of Hartmann's works (1962, 76). In it the author says nothing of himself, his rank, and his search for an appropriate poetic source, as he is wont to do in the prologues of his other works. Nor is the style of this prologue characterized by the even-flowing, well-punctuated, and generally restrained tone of other prologues, but rather by the less- considered syntax of daily speech and by a "style of emotional proclamation" that reminds one of a sermon. Agreeing with Zwierzina's (1893) position that the prologue is genuinely that of Hartmann, Wapnewski is among those who consider that it can be seen as a personal confession on the part of the author (1962, 77). A position supported by this understanding of the prologue is that Hartmann, deeply affected by the death of his lord and patron, has turned his attention away from the frivolous worldly works of his youth (i.e., the *Klage, Erec,* early lyrics in the tradition of high *minne*) and toward matters of greater spiritual depth in his next narrative works, *Gregorius* and *Der arme Heinrich,* and in his Crusade songs. Others have dismissed Hartmann's reference to the sinful works of youth as a literary commonplace (Schwietering 1921, 203), while another approach is to view this reference as a generic marker, which prepares the audience for a work of a religious/spiritual kind (Cormeau and Störmer 1985, 128). This would indicate not a deep crisis in the life of the author, but rather a shift from a worldly to a spiritual *literary* undertaking (cf. also Mertens 1978a, 78–79).

The worldly element in Hartmann's poem has been the object of critical attention focusing on the material used by Hartmann in his tale, independent of the work's interpretation within a theological framework. Sparnaay draws attention to what he sees as the basic knightly structure upon which *Gregorius* is based: "Knighthood forms the foundation of the story" (1920, 15). This story shares the following features with Arthurian tales: the summoning of a council of the potentates, the council of the father to the son, the yearning of an inexperienced youngster for knightly activity, and, most notably, the liberation of a princess under siege (7). These similarities indicated for Sparnaay in this early essay that *Gregorius* is basically Arthurian but that it was strongly transformed by "theological motifs" in the direction of a legend (16).

Although typically regarded as corresponding to the genre that deals with saints' lives (i.e., *legenda*), the likelihood that this work was produced for a lay audience and not for the expected monastic audience of the *legenda*, when combined with a kind of theological thought that is not easily identifiable, makes the identification of genre difficult. Along with the majority of later scholars, Barthel (1854, 34) and Scherer (1883, 182) stated simply that *Gregorius* is a *legenda*. Schönbach followed suit: "Hartmann considered his work as a legend, not as a courtly-worldly story, and this is the way it was received by his contemporaries, as the two Latin translations and the inclusion of the story in saints' lives demonstrate" (1894, 450). For Wapnewski, Hartmann's work is a legend, the purpose of which is to demonstrate God's grace in an extreme case of human sinfulness (1962, 80). Mertens states that *Gregorius* is a novelty of genre history in the German context, since there is no clear literary tradition into which it clearly fits (1978a, 21), and Dahlgrün offers a similar opinion (1991, 111). Jackson considers *Gregorius* "something of an experiment, a mixture of religious legend and courtly romance both in structure and in social function" (1994, 166). Today scholars typically refer to *Gregorius* and *Der arme Heinrich* as Hartmann's legendary works, while recognizing that the term *legenda* is being used very loosely.

The structure of *Gregorius* has been considered somewhat more difficult to identify than that of Hartmann's other works. According to Wapnewski, *Gregorius* lacks a structure that could be considered a part of the poetic plan or that itself contributes to the message of Hartmann's work (1962, 83). Wapnewski contents himself with a simple division of the tale into a prologue, an initial excursion (*Ausfahrt*) that lasts from the infant Gregorius's being consigned to the waves to his discovery that he is an orphan, a subsequent excursion that culminates in the mother-son incest, a third excursion that brings Gregorius to the rock upon which he does penance and ultimately to his salvation, and a fourth and final excursion, to become pope in Rome and to be reunited with his mother. Mertens sees in *Gregorius* the same bipartite structure that is visible in the Arthurian works. In *Gregorius* the two structural segments correspond roughly to two identities: *Rex justus,* after knightly endeavors, and *Pontifex justus,* upon completion of penance (1978a, 71). Plate (1983) is critical both of Eggers's 1956 attempt, based on number symbolism, to define a middle point of the text that serves as the axis of a symmetrical composition and of the frequent attempt to define the structure of the work in terms of a variation of the *Doppelwegstruktur* that is seen to underlie Hartmann's Arthurian works (by Mertens, above, and Hirschberg 1979; Plate is generally critical of what he calls "the almost fashionable interpretation scheme of the *Doppelkreis-Struktur* in the visions of the so-called Munich School," 8). Instead, Plate posits a three-part structure based on the revolution of the wheel of fortune (6). In each of these parts Plate detects four positions, corresponding to an initial point of departure, a descent or fall, the nadir, and a return to good fortune: I) 1. Gregorius is born noble; 2. He is placed upon the waters; 3. Gregorius is "der ellende weise" [the abandoned orphan]; 4. Gregorius receives the name of the abbot. II) 1. Gregorius is an exemplary pupil in the abbey; 2. Gregorius strikes his step brother; 3. the foster mother scolds Gregorius and reveals he is a foundling; 4. Gregorius feels called to be a knight. III) 1. Gregorius proves himself to be an accomplished knight and prince; 2) The mother recognizes her son in her husband; 3. Gregorius does penance on the rock; 4. Gregorius is summoned to Rome to be pope.

The problem at the core of *Gregorius,* judging by this work's critical reception, is that of Gregorius's sinfulness. Most of the other problems discussed by critics (the meaning of the prologue; the significance of Gregorius's knightly activity; free will or lack thereof in the hero; the significance of his unusual penance) are linked in one way or another to this central issue. In the criticism of Hartmann's other works, sinfulness per se is seldom an issue, since this implies an overtly theological framework that may be foreign to Hartmann's literary designs; instead, scholars prefer to speak of guilt (*Schuld*). In the case of *Gregorius,* a work that seems much more overtly religious in its concerns — for example in its use of religious terms such as *buoze* [penance] and *bîhte* [confession] in the prologue — there has been less reluctance to speak more specifically of sin (although the word *Schuld* continues often to be used more or less synonymously for *Sünde* [sin]) and to search the work for that critical moment when Gregorius brings sin upon himself. This interpretive approach, which tends to view Hartmann's work primarily in theological terms, has recently been countered, as we shall see, by other critics who posit in different ways that the meaning of Hartmann's work is distorted if it is seen as a theological treatise rather than as a work of literature that was, in all likelihood, produced for an audience consisting primarily of lay nobles. The result of the critical debate on the question of guilt/sin has been, in the words of Tobin, "myriad and conflicting opinions" (1973, 67).

Barthel considered *Gregorius* to be an "artistically complicated story," the purpose of which was to demonstrate the miraculous power of God's grace (1854, 41). Despite his admiration of this purpose, Barthel's basically Romantic sensitivities were disturbed by what he regarded as contrived elements that spoiled enjoyment of the poem. First, the work was marked by such a crass theory of original sin that it could not avoid being offensive to "the children of our time" (41). Barthel is further disturbed by the repetition of incest, which he interprets not symbolically, but according to the standard of realism as something that could never happen in real life (41). The foundation of subsequent *Gregorius* scholarship was established in the studies of Schönbach (1894). Although Schönbach devotes himself to analyses of all of Hartmann's works, his interest in the medieval author begins with the establishment of Hartmann's religious views, particularly as these are expressed in *Gregorius*. Perhaps due to this interest, Schönbach ends by viewing *Gregorius* as the most important of Hartmann's legends and by making his evaluation of all of Hartmann's work dependent on an understanding of this work. Schönbach was the first to link *Gregorius* with the theological literature (e.g., Peter of Poitiers, the sentences of Peter Lombard) of the High Middle Ages. On the basis of such theological texts, Schönbach arrived at a conclusion that was of great importance for subsequent interpretations: Gregorius is free from sin — at least from the standpoint of the Church — both in the case of his parents' incest and in his own incest with his mother, since sin, according to official church doctrine, consisted both in the sinful act itself and in a willful disposition (*voluntas*) to commit the act. Gregorius does not sin, according to Schönbach, because he lacks this wilful disposition (1894, 102): Gregorius does not sin for he transgresses *unknowingly*.

Another element entering into Hartmann's work were popular beliefs, according to which Gregorius was tainted by sin in both instances of incest. Schönbach posits that Hartmann ultimately follows his French source in connecting Gregorius's long and unusually severe atonement with these popular beliefs (102). Schönbach's interpretation thus suggests that Hartmann's work contains two aspects, one connected to religious literature with which Hartmann was familiar, the other to popular traditions concerning incest. Although both of these aspects have validity in themselves, they are not, according to Schönbach, reconciled well in Hartmann's work. It is notable that Schönbach considers penance, and not Gregorius's problematical sinfulness, to be the theme of the work: "the importance of the inner-transformation of the hero recedes, and the main weight falls on the external penance, the atonement in self-chastisement that is adopted of one's own free will" (1894, 449). Later critics were reluctant to accept the proposition that Gregorius's penance could not be understood in theological terms as the result of a definable sin (perhaps because falling back on popular notions to explain it seemed to deny conceptual consistency or closure to Hartmann's poem); many were also unwilling to accept Schönbach's thesis that the theme is the external penance rather than sinfulness and inner transformation.

Hauck (1922) was among the first to have problems with Schönbach's view that Gregorius's penance cannot be linked to a theologically definable sin. For Hauck, who insists on a theologically coherent conception, Hartmann ultimately fails to solve the problem his work poses: it is not possible from a theological standpoint to reconcile the fact that Gregorius desires what is good and right and entrusts himself to God's providence (e.g., when he leaves the cloister), with the unspeakable sin to which his entirely positive attitude leads (554). The endeavor to define the work in terms of a consistent theological conception was resumed in many articles and monographs of the fifties, possibly as an aspect of a more general preoccupation with *Schuld* in the postwar years. Schieb (1950) and Nobel (1957) begin with the assumption that the conspicuously religious prologue — particularly the parable of the good Samaritan — can be seen as an allegorical anticipation of the action of the tale and therefore as a key to understanding it (Schieb considers, for example, that Hartmann here warns about *vürgedank* [*praesumptio*]), and both critics ultimately detect an attitude of self-aggrandizement (*superbia*) in Gregorius that is the inner sin which ultimately leads to the incest with his mother. This sinful attitude is for both Schieb and Nobel most visible in Gregorius's presumed failure, because of his desire for worldly deeds, to follow the advice of his mother as transmitted on the tablet. Nobel even considers that Hartmann's prologue contains direct translations from theological literature (1957, 44). In an article that demonstrates many similarities to the views of Schieb and Nobel, Kuhn (1953) found "a deep inner guilt" (Kuhn uses the word *Schuld*, [guilt] and not *Sünde* [sin]) in Gregorius's prideful trust in himself and in the mother's sinful doubt about God's providence (*desperatio*), both of which become tangible at the moment when mother and son have discovered their incest. In contrast to Schieb and Nobel, Kuhn's interpretation implies not a dependence on theological literature, but rather a "poetic symbolism" at the heart of Hartmann's work. Hartmann, according to Kuhn, "destroys . . . the normal fixed justice of God and the world, trust in one's own action, and dependence on guilt and penance, in order to build up a new and deeper human attitude" (81). As pointed out by Gössmann in her review of critical literature dealing with the question of guilt in *Gregorius* from 1950 to 1971 (1974), Kuhn's position changes later on (cf. Kuhn 1959a, 172), hovering between a more strictly theological and a more strictly poetic conception of Hartmann's work; although this draws Gössmann's criticism, Kuhn's perceived wavering in fact corresponds well to the actual constitution of Hartmann's work, which might be seen as manifesting a similar wavering. Another interpretation positing the theologically programmatic character of the prologue, and sinful pride on the part of Gregorius, is the dissertation of Ohly (1958), who, like Schieb and Nobel, sees the fault most tangibly expressed in Gregorius's neglect of his mother's wish, recorded on the tablet, that he pray and atone for the sin of his parents. In the opinion of Ohly, the two paths described by Hartmann in the prologue of this work provide the key not just for the interpretation of this work, but also for understanding all of Hartmann's narrative poems; thus, in a manner similar to Schönbach, Ohly makes the conspicuously religious tone of the *Gregorius* prologue the foundation of a theological approach to all of Hartmann's works. The essay of Willson (1959) is in many respects exemplary of the prevalent theological line of interpretation. Beginning with the assumption that the parable of the good Samaritan in the prologue establishes a religious program that is consistently followed in the body of the work, Willson eventually finds Gregorius guilty of sin in a manner that is similar to previous critics:

> Gregorius's departure from the cloister in which he is brought up marks the beginning of his own road to *superbia* . . . Had he remained in the cloister, he would have shown his love for God and respect for his Divine Order, and the sin of his parents would not have been visited upon him to the extent of a second incestual relationship (198–99).

In the sixties one observes increased criticism of the idea that Hartmann's work is more or less directly dependent on theological literature. King (1963) was among the first to voice skepticism about the idea that *Gregorius* can or should be appraised in terms of the theological writings of Hartmann's age. Pointing to the prominent worldly elements in both *Der arme Heinrich* and in *Gregorius* — which are *not,* in the view of King, presented merely in order to be rejected — King posits that one cannot conclude that the prominent spiritual focus of these two works represents a rejection or a negation of the created world (314–15). Rejecting the interpretations of Schieb (1950) and Nobel (1957), which had found fault with Gregorius's decision to become a knight and with his consequent neglect of his mother's wish that he pray for the soul of his father, King argues that the nature of Gregorius's penance is not proportionate to a sin of this scale, that the mother's instructions on the tablet are not at all clear, and that Gregorius, even as knight, conscientiously reads the tablet and prays for his parents every day (318–21). The recurrence of incest, which Hartmann along with his audience would have understood according to popular notions and not according to theological precepts, is not a result of his decision to become a knight; such an indictment of knighthood is not possible for King, in view of Hartmann's entirely positive portrayal of the hero's knightly exploits (321). A lesson of the story, that knighthood is connected with "great dangers" (340), does not mitigate the basically positive conception of knighthood in the work. The problem is not in Gregorius as an individual; it is rather "in the system" (323). In the final analysis the work presents in King's view the "great dangers" inherent in being a knight, without however wishing in any way to question the validity and worth of this worldly order (340–41).

Wapnewski adopts the position that guilt is to be found in Gregorius's failure to do penance for his parents, but at the same time he stresses the work's essentially poetic character by positing that *Gregorius* is a "dismantling of the values of the courtly world" but not a complete dismantling (1962, 87). The message of *Gregorius* is that courtly values in and of themselves are insufficient and in need of a higher justification. The work is thus seen in the context of all of Hartmann's works, and not as an isolated theological treatise. Although arriving ultimately at the standard conclusion that Gregorius makes himself guilty of *superbia*, Wolf (1964) differs from earlier religious interpretations by positing three distinct levels in the work: 1) the basic story of incest; 2) a courtly actualization of this story from the perspective of the latter twelfth century; and 3) a final religious formation. The epic narrative of the courtly section extends to the moment in which Gregorius and his mother discover their incestuous relationship. At this point the epic narrative of the courtly level recedes, and the religious formation — which includes the penance and Gregorius's rise to the papacy — begins to occur (19). Wolf thus implies a variation of the idea of different textual layers that was originally put forward by Schönbach. He also rejects the idea of a direct dependence on theological literature, even if he ultimately puts forward a strongly religious interpretation. The poetic character of *Gregorius* is also stressed in Schwarz's (1964) essay on free will, which rejects the idea that Hartmann followed any particular theological source (e.g., such as Abelard), only to posit in the end that the conception of this work was determined by an Augustinian conception of sin (i.e., turning away from the higher divine good toward a lower worldly good in his departure from the cloister) with which all medieval Christians would have been familiar. Although this essay remains strongly theological, the idea that Hartmann slavishly followed a particular source (or sources) has given way to a broader cultural conception of the religious thought by which he may have been influenced: "one should analyze the text of the poem without being burdened by the weight of thought, not found in *Gregorius*" (131).

The turn away from the more strictly theological approach to Hartmann's work becomes more pronounced in the books of Cormeau and Dittmann, both published in 1966. On the basis of a more precise and detailed analysis of the literature of early Scholasticism, Cormeau arrives at a much more cautious estimation of its likely influence on *Gregorius*. Against one of the dominant trends of earlier criticism, Cormeau rejects the idea that the prologue contains the key for understanding the work as a whole in theological terms (101–3). More important, he rejects the idea that Gregorius incurs any sort of subjective guilt/sin. Gregorius's guilt is not subjective and personal; all statements made by Hartmann with reference to Gregorius's qualities and intentions are (as previously pointed out by Zuntz and King) consistently positive. Correspondingly, no fault can be found in any specific action, such as Gregorius's departure from the cloister; on the contrary, only by leaving the cloister and embarking on a knighthood in service of God can the program of the work — greatest sin, severest penance, eternal life — be realized. Gregorius's guilt/sin cannot be located in any specific thought or action, because it is objective rather than subjective or personal. This is the way that Cormeau understands the apparent paradox of the "good sinner": subjectively Gregorius is good, free of sin, and even exemplary, but objectively he is, as is all mankind, sinful and dependent on the redemptive power of God's grace. Gregorius's rise to the papacy in the end is a logical culmination of this dynamic. It occurs because he, in an exemplary manner, freely accepts the objective guilt as his own and does penance for it. This amounts to a "giving up of self" (*Selbstaufgabe*) for which God raises Gregorius to the greatest heights (72–73). Dittmann also considers a direct influence of the literature of early Scholasticism unlikely: "Whether Hartmann ever read Petrus Lombardus is beside the point (although I consider it unlikely) . . ." (1966, 183). Like Cormeau, Dittmann argues against the programmatic character of the prologue and the idea of a specific subjective guilt/sin on the part of Gregorius, who remains in every respect exemplary and brings objective sin upon himself through no individual failing (i.e., no *superbia*). Dittmann also contributes the thesis that Hartmann in this work advocates an older but still popular definition of atonement, in which the act of atonement itself — without the mediation of instances of the Church — sufficed to reconcile the Christian with God, and that the author pits this earlier conception against that of early Scholasticism, which stresses the act of confession of sins before a priest. Seigfried's essay from 1971 suggests a weakness in these and other interpretations that reject the idea of personal guilt/sin on the part of Gregorius. Basing his definitions on the work itself, rather than on hypothetical connections to theological literature, Seigfried argues that the work itself presents a simple conception: Gregorius desires the course of action that ultimately proves to be sinful, therefore he sins, and his sinfulness is not mitigated by his inability to know where his actions would lead.

Interpretation of Gregorius also affirms the assumption of individual guilt/sin in the 1973 interpretation of Tobin. In a review and critique of previous interpretations, particularly those of Cormeau and Dittmann, Tobin argues that a rejection of individual guilt leaves much of the work unexplained:

> the question of guilt cannot be pushed completely into a corner because it is not simply a question which is hermetically sealed off from other basic questions in *Gregorius*. Inseparably bound up with it is the picture of man which Hartmann gives us and also, ulti-

mately, Hartmann's way of interpreting the whole of reality including God. (57)

Although rejecting the position of earlier critics that Gregorius is guilty of *superbia* (70), it is something close to this sin that Tobin seems to be describing when he views the hero as guilty of "a falsely idealistic image of man which is not willing to admit weaknesses and insufficiencies" (72). This faulty image of man's abilities becomes especially tangible in Gregorius's departure from the cloister ("his [incestuous] origin really makes such a life impossible"; 73) and in the recognition scene with his mother, in which Gregorius at first mistakenly assumes that it is the nobility of his birth, rather than his sinful origin, that is at issue (73). Within the framework of a study that is based on the assumption that Hartmann's works articulate dualistic or gradualistic modes of thought, *Gregorius* is ultimately seen as profoundly dualistic (whereas in the presumably later work, *Der arme Heinrich*, Tobin posits that Hartmann has moved beyond the dualism visible in *Gregorius* to a gradualistic conception of the world and God). This interpretation, like that of Seigfried, bases its arguments primarily on the work itself and not on more or less direct connections to theological literature.

In her 1974 review of the critical literature on the question of Gregorius's guilt/sin from 1950 to 1971, Gössmann adds important observations of her own, particularly that the gradual movement away from a strictly theological interpretation of *Gregorius* toward an understanding of it on its own (poetic) terms was due largely to increasing skepticism about the previously assumed connection between the starkly religious prologue and the body of the work (Gössmann sees this skepticism as beginning with Wapnewski) (78). Gössmann points out that the strictly theological approach is deprived of its most important element, if the prologue, as has been asserted by some critics, was not even a part of the original work, but rather added by a later scribe. It is noteworthy, however, that the movement away from the strictly theological interpretation has continued, even as most critics have continued to consider the prologue as a part of Hartmann's original work.

A mixture of older and newer tendencies is visible in the study of Goebel (1974). On the one hand, Goebel proposes to view the work solely on the basis of its poetic structure. Focusing on what he calls the "classical scheme" of departure and reunion (121), affecting in this instance Gregorius and his mother, Goebel points out as a structuring principle a doubling of this scheme (i.e., 1. abandonment of Gregorius, reunion in marriage of Gregorius and his mother; 2. departure after the discovery of incest, reunion subsequent to mother's confession to Pope Gregorius). On the other hand, this classical structure is seen in theological terms that are reminiscent of past interpretations. Not only does the second level correct the first (121), but Gregorius's departure from the cloister and his mother's decision to marry despite an earlier vow to the contrary are seen as moments that retard progress toward the second happy reunion. These decisions are consequently viewed, as they were in earlier interpretations, as sins on the part of Gregorius (although in a broad biblical sense and not with respect to the ideas of early Scholasticism) that anticipate and lead to the greater sin of incest with his mother. Another position taken by Goebel, which is worthy of mention in this context because it has been a point on which scholars have disagreed, is that Gregorius's departure into the world involved a breaking of vows that bound him to the cloister for life. Other scholars (cf. Mertens 1978a, 64–67) have posited that practice with respect to oblates differed according to time and place, so that it is difficult to establish if Gregorius's departure would have been considered sinful in this regard.

In many respects, the study of Mertens (1978a) involves a turn away from the usual focus on the question of the hero's guilt (for Mertens, the focal point is the hero's atonement) and, in its sociological orientation, from the traditional manner of argumentation based on interpretation from theological texts (or on the rejection thereof). Following the research of historians such as Borst (1973), Mertens argues that Hartmann's work can be understood in terms of a form of life (*Lebensform*) with which a noble audience of the twelfth century would have been familiar: the eremite. Based on historical figures such as William Firmat, Robert of Arbrissel, Bernhard of Thiron, and Vatalis of Savigny, Mertens points out that the eremitic life form, which rejects the physical comforts of society and pursues an extreme asceticism in the wastelands far from civilization, can be understood as an extreme form of penance that is undertaken by the eremite of his own free will. This penance does not correspond to any particular identifiable transgression; rather, it presents itself as "spontaneous and gratuitous" (50). Mertens sees the basic contours of this life form in Hartmann's work. Like the eremite Gregorius's decision to undertake his penance on the rock cannot be identified with a specific sin, since he not guilty of any such sin according to the theological thinking of his day. Gregorius, in this view, is not somehow guilty for the sin of his parents; he is not guilty in his wish to leave the abbey and undertake knightly deeds (Mertens notes that Hartmann gives no indication that the abbot has won the argument with Gregorius about the latter's decision to become a knight) (64–67); he commits no sin for the incestuous relationship with his mother. Hence, his penance is spontaneous and gratuitous, corresponding to no rule book, but rather to a profound personal sense of sinfulness. Also in its extreme asceticism and in its location in the wilds far from civilization, Gregorius's penance on the rock corresponds to the eremitic life form. Mertens sees this act of penance ultimately as a representative act: Gregorius does not so much embrace unintended and unforeseen sin as his own (cf. Cormeau), as he takes the sinfulness of mankind upon himself in imitation of Christ. His penance therefore has both a personal and a (possibly more significant) social aspect (58–70).

Henne (1982) proposes an approach to *Gregorius* which is similar to that of Mertens in its sociological orientation. Henne views the work as an allegorical portrayal of the struggle between two different kinds of religiosity: the abbot represents the traditional Benedictine, while Gregorius acts continually according to the logic of the Cluniac and Gregorian reform movements of the eleventh and twelfth centuries (156). The latter is ultimately successful — and rises to the papacy — because he adheres to reformist ideal of spirituality outside of existing church institutions. The importance of the historically documented eremitic form of life, which had been pointed out by Mertens, is given a more specific meaning in Henne's interpretation: "Gregorius's eremitic life is a rejection of the cloister, the traditional place of religious life, which his abbot had urged him to accept" (163). Henne sees Gregorius's guilt as consistent with this reading of the work: notable is Gregorius's strong sense of personal transgression, which is consistent with the spirituality of the reform movement and not with ordered structure of traditional cloister life. In the end Gregorius's guilt is seen as significant, not as an example in itself, but because of the unorthodox kind of atonement to which it leads: "with his penance Gregorius atones for the social guilt of a church become worldly" (185).

The article of Kühnel (1985) points out in *Gregorius* the traditional structure of the *legenda* (sin, contrition, atonement, and grace), posits that Gregorius's knightly adventures occupy the structural position corresponding to sin, and arrives at a conclusion that is similar to the previous appraisal of Wapnewski: "Hartmann's tale of *Gregorius* is actually a work that is critical of culture and civilization, that places the developing courtly culture in question and dismantles its ideals — perhaps from the perspective of older religious culture and literature" (163). Spiewok's 1989 article focuses first on conflicting ideologies in all of Hartmann's works: on the one hand, there is an affirmation of the worldly values of feudal-aristocratic society (e.g., in the Arthurian works); on the other, there is a negation of these values (in the legends). It is this conflict that we also see within *Gregorius*, the simple lesson of which is that life in the created world implicates man in sin (133). One can avoid guilt only in absolute negation of this world ("absoluter Weltverneinung") (134). Clark's appraisal of *Gregorius*, with its abstract focus on mind — which in contrast to most studies does not endeavor to establish the relationship of the poem to the religiosity of Hartmann's time, posits the theme of knowledge as an overarching principle "that unifies the poem's involved cycle of losing and finding, hiding and revealing, forgetting and remembering, and, ultimately, sin and redemption" (1989, 90).

Dahlgrün's study of Hartmann's *Gregorius* and *Der arme Heinrich* departs from the assumption that these two works can be seen within the framework of the religious reform movements of the eleventh and twelfth centuries. In contrast to Henne, who operated with a similar frame of reference, Dahlgrün stresses the phenomenon of lay religiosity, of which Hartmann can be viewed as a contributing representative (1991, 62). Dahlgrün argues that Gregorius atones for the unknown incest, but takes an unusually extreme position in asserting that he is guilty neither of a subjective, personal guilt nor of an objective guilt as representative of fallen mankind. This position, like many earlier ones, seeks to enlarge the discrepancy between transgression and atonement by diminishing the former almost to the point of disappearance. Notable also is Dahlgrün's opinion — which stands in stark contrast to those of Kühnel and Spiewok — that Hartmann's appraisal of courtly ideals is ambivalent, that there is neither a clear rejection of worldly ideals nor an unconditional affirmation of them (177). The more recent appraisal of Jackson shows no signs of a revival of the dualistic condemnation of worldly values in this work. Following the appraisal of Cormeau, Jackson sees *Gregorius* in terms of "a critical scrutiny, but not a fundamental rejection, of secular values" (1994, 166).

Gregorius is clearly Hartmann's most overtly religious work. In it one observes a fundamental shift away from the worldly themes visible in the *Klage* and in the Arthurian works. Despite the uniqueness of this work, this cross section of the criticism dealing with the most central problem in *Gregorius* — the hero's guilt/sin or lack thereof — indicates increasing skepticism about the applicability of a strictly religious/theological frame of reference. "It is easy," Schwarz has said of theological interpretations of *Gregorius*, "to read into the poem views which the poet did not or could not know, or did not wish to express" (1984, 130). This skepticism about the relevance of theological ideas to the understanding of *Gregorius* amounts in many cases to a rejection of the idea that there is a specific identifiable guilt on the part of Gregorius for which he must atone (such guilt, as we have seen, has frequently been connected to Gregorius's career as a knight) and even to the postulation that every step Gregorius takes (especially this knightly segment) is, in some way or another, positive and necessary in order to achieve the happy culmination of the work. If Hartmann produced this work for the same kind of audience that could find enjoyment in works such as *Erec* and *Iwein*, as is generally assumed, then it seems inappropriate to place *Gregorius* (alone or along with *Der arme Heinrich*) in a relationship of opposition or rejection to the worldly works. Even if one observes more or less pronounced signs of a dualistic logic in this work, *Gregorius* would seem to be already grounded in a courtly/knightly culture for which such a logic may mean something other than contempt for the created world.

6: *Der arme Heinrich*

THE COMPLETE WORK, with little more than 1500 verses Hartmann's shortest narrative, is preserved in three manuscripts. The fourteenth-century manuscript of Strasbourg (A) was destroyed in 1870 but survives in a copy made in 1784. There is also the fourteenth-century Heidelberg redaction (B), which diverges significantly from A, and the Kolozcaer manuscript (K), also known as Bb, which is close to B. In addition there are three fragments: 61 verses in St. Florian (C) from the thirteenth century, 117 verses in Indersdorf (D) from the fourteenth century, and 117 verses in Benediktbeuren (E) from the thirteenth century. The complete manuscripts present two widely divergent versions of the work (e.g., in the B strand of the transmission Heinrich and the girl do not consummate the marriage but withdraw to a monastic life), which complicates its edition and interpretation. Since A, which is considered closest to Hartmann's original work, was composed more than a century later, modern editions are, at best, an educated guess about Hartmann's original(s). The source of this work is not known. *Der arme Heinrich* may be related to two Latin exempla from the fourteenth and fifteenth centuries — *Heinricus pauper* and *Albertus pauper* — but the exact nature of the relationship has remained unclear, although a Latin source is likely, given that Hartmann in the prologue of this work stresses his literacy when speaking of his search through "mislîchen buochen" [various books] for a suitable tale. It will be difficult if not impossible to locate a specific source, if, as has been posited (Mertens 1978a, 56), Hartmann took only some of the elements from a story he knew and combined them with elements from personal experience in order to give literary justification to a marriage that lowered the social standing of the family of his lord(s)/patron(s) or of his own family (critics have moved progressively from the former to the latter view, according to Cormeau and Störmer 1985, 33–34). Such a theory might explain the marriage between the noble Heinrich and the peasant girl at the end of the work, which is contrary to legal and social practice and to standard literary usage, in which the equality of birth of marriage partners is the norm; Sparnaay (1938), for example, considers that the marriage was certainly historical (2).

As difficult as the identification of the source has been the definition of the genre to which *Der arme Heinrich* belongs. Gervinus (1853) calls it a "schwäbische Volkslegende" [popular Swabian legend] (364). Scherer (1883) calls it a "pious story" (182). Although frequently designated today as a *höfische Legende* [courtly legend] (Frenzel 1953, 36), Hartmann's tale also shows elements of the novella, the fairy tale, and the exemplum. This mixture of elements has led some to doubt the possibility of an entirely satisfactory definition of the work's genre (Könneker 1987, 52–53).

Der arme Heinrich is by far the best known of Hartmann's works outside the scholarly community. The poetic language of this work has been praised in much the same way as *Iwein,* with many critics (recently Arndt 1980) suggesting, on the basis of its formal and stylistic excellence, that it — and not *Iwein* — was Hartmann's last work and crowning achievement. *Der arme Heinrich* has appeared in many translations from the early nineteenth century to the present and has been reworked in prose, poetry, and drama by writers such as Adelbert Chamisso, Conrad Ferdinand Meyer, Ricarda Huch, and Gerhart Hauptmann (cf. Rautenberg 1985, 94–95, and Sparre 1988, 152–53). The studies of Tardel (1905), Rautenberg, and Sparre have shed light on the long and rich history of this work's reception by authors and critics alike. For Tardel, *Der arme Heinrich* represents a reworking of two of the oldest themes in Western literature, which first present themselves in Sophocles's *Philoctetes* and the biblical story of Job: the debilitating effects of disease and the seemingly inscrutable affliction of man by God. Tardel's study, in large part a tribute to the works of Gerhart Hauptmann and Ricarda Huch, posits that Hartmann's work makes an important addition to the story of Job: by transforming the originally inscrutable affliction into a punishment for the worldly orientation of Heinrich, God is "excused for his superhuman severity" (2). Many decades later Kaiser picks up Tardel's discussion of Hartmann's work, points to the same literary ancestors, and posits that *Der arme Heinrich* stands in a broader literary tradition extending from *Philoctetes* to Thomas Mann's *Der Zauberberg,* in which disease functions to increase man's sensitivity to the basic questions of his existence (1964, 37).

The study of Rautenberg focuses on the nineteenth-century reception of Hartmann's work, which was very much shaped by the early edition/translation of the Grimm brothers published in 1815. Consistent with the Romantic inclinations and the increasing national sentiment of the Napoleonic years, the Grimms' edition/translation casts the work somewhat analogously to the *Nibelungenlied* as a folk tale. Conspicuous is the desire to see Hartmann as a poet who articulated values emerging naturally and spontaneously from the German people — which were concentrated in what was seen as the young maiden's selfless and loyal love. The lifeblood of the maiden, given out of love to cure Heinrich of his leprosy, becomes in the Grimms' edition and subsequent appraisals of the work, after the emancipation of German territories from French occupation, symbolic of broader interests in the fragmented German lands. The historically myopic view that originally helped to entrench Hartmann's work in modern German culture is visible in the foreword to the Grimms' edition:

> Now our entire Fatherland has in its blood healed itself of the French leprosy and regained youthful vigor. May every German henceforth pay such a price and be always prepared happily to sacrifice himself.

Sparre's study posits that the reception of Hartmann's work was facilitated and shaped by two broader thematic concerns of fin de siècle literature: yearning for death and redemption in love. These two themes, which represent a polarity of *eros* and *thanatos,* were, in the view of Sparre, addressed particularly well by the subject matter of Hartmann's *Der arme Heinrich* and Gottfried von Straßburg's *Tristan*. Interesting with respect to the literary reception of the medieval works is skepticism on the part of Sparre about how well the subject matter of the medieval works serves as the vehicle of expression for modern concerns (201–2 and 241–42).

Early literary critics operated much under the influence of the Grimms' appraisal of *Der arme Heinrich* as a folk tale. Barthel's glowing recommendation of this work is clearly based on this kind of view: "Seldom has a poet been so open to the childlike spirit of the folk tale" (1854, 43). For Barthel the work contained "etwas eigenthümlich Schwärmerisches" [something uniquely rapturous] (49); from it flowed "a clear heaven of innocence and devotion" (43). Barthel considers this work to be conceptually coherent, in contrast to be the random adventuring of the heroes of the Arthurian works (43), even if one has to overlook the miraculous healing of Heinrich and the girl as a concession to the "spirit of the Middle Ages" (49–50). Traces of the Romantic ethos are still present in much later appraisals, such as that of Sparnaay, who considered that *Der arme Heinrich*, Hartmann's greatest literary achievement, touches us — as none of Hartmann's other works — with the "Hauch überzeitlicher Poesie" (breath of timeless poetry) (1938, 1). The recognition of other genre elements in this work besides those of the folk tale and hence of the possibility that this work may be a sophisticated artistic construction on the part of the poet Hartmann has in this century accompanied the increasingly tendency to praise this work on the basis of its formal and aesthetic quality and the clarity of its language, which are, according to de Boor (1953), achieved "with all of the means of Hartmann's mature art" (78). The distance of many current appraisals from the immediacy of early Romantic ones is visible in Könneker's 1987 appraisal of Hartmann's language in *Der arme Heinrich* as characterized by a high degree of abstraction (59).

The structure of *Der arme Heinrich* has been divided by Fechter (1955) into three parts, a short frame at the beginning and at the end, and a longer middle section: 1) Sir Heinrich, 2) Poor Heinrich, and 3) the good Sir Heinrich. The transitions between the frames and the longer central section are clearly marked by divine actions: the illness from God and God's healing of Heinrich and the girl. A more elaborate conception of the work's structure was proposed by Fourquet (1961), who divides the work into fourteen narrative blocks, each consisting of four *Abschnitte* [sections]. The work thus manifests, according to Fourquet, who follows in this essay the kind of structural analysis made popular by Eggers (1956), a consistent and harmonious proportion that is also visible in other literary works of Hartmann's age. Asher (1984), basing himself on Kuhn's observation of a doubling of motifs in Hartmann's *Erec*, finds the same principle at work as a structuring principle in *Der arme Heinrich*. The first instance of *Motivverdoppelung* (e.g., Heinrich's inner suffering after being stricken by illness) prepares the listener for the increased intensity and climactic character of the second (the maiden's suffering after Heinrich rejects her sacrifice). Instances of such motif doubling, which takes a variety of different forms, contribute, according to Asher, to the structural and narrative coherence of Hartmann's work (323).

Whatever Hartmann's immediate sources were, it is clear that he availed himself of popular and learned traditions concerning the nature of leprosy and the healing power of human blood. The popular layer was recognized by the Grimm brothers and other early critics such as Barthel (1854), who pointed out that lepers were social outcasts, that leprosy was widespread in Europe during Hartmann's lifetime, and that lepers had to live alone in the countryside in miserable huts, warning passersby of their presence by ringing a bell. Wlislocki drew attention to popular beliefs in the healing power of human blood in the folk tales and lore of Rumania and the Balkans, positing that Hartmann may have based his tale on such a popular folk tale, the oldest version of which is probably to be sought in the Orient (1890, 225). Significant with respect to the significance of Hartmann's work is the medieval view of leprosy as both a physical and a spiritual malady: "The leper was someone who has been stricken by God" (Könneker 1987, 18). The physical symptoms of the disease made manifest to the medieval mind the sinfulness of the inner soul, as is clear in Caesarius of Heisterbach's distinction of three different kinds of leprosy, indicative of heresy, schism, and simony respectively (Henne 1982, 187). Könneker notes that human blood was long felt to have a curative effect, from the *Historia Naturalis* of Pliny in the first century A.D., which reported that Egyptians used human blood for healing purposes, to the sixteenth-century physician Paracelsus, who recommended blood as a cure for leprosy; this belief was probably originally connected to ancient cultic practices that never completely died out, even after the Commandments for Jews and Christ's sacrifice for Christians had in theory removed the necessity of the blood sacrifice (Könneker 1987, 18). Although the influence on Hartmann's work of the popular and learned views of leprosy in the Middle Ages is recognized in most scholarly appraisals, the relevance of these views for the interpretation of Hartmann's work remains difficult to ascertain. A treatment of the symbolic significance of leprosy in Hartmann's work (as indicative of Heinrich's sinful pride) is contained in the broader study of leprosy in medieval literature by Brody (1974).

Beliefs about leprosy and its cure by means of a blood sacrifice existed during Hartmann's day in two literary traditions. One, the so-called Sylvester legend, is linked to the Roman emperor Constantine, who, after contracting leprosy, forgoes the sacrifice of young boys to achieve a cure. Subsequently he is healed in the sacrament of baptism administered by Pope Sylvester. The other tradition, the story of Amicus and Amelius, focuses on the selflessness of the individual who has to make the sacrifice. Konrad von Würzburg's *Engelhart,* for example, presents a situation in which the protagonist sacrifices his children to achieve the cure of a friend. After the cure is achieved, the children are miraculously restored to life. It is possible that Hartmann's source had already combined these two traditions, but it is also conceivable, especially lacking such a source, that the combination was Hartmann's own achievement (cf. Cormeau and Störmer 1985, 150). Hartmann's combination of these two themes, in the view of many critics, achieves a previously lacking ethical dimension and a greater individual depth. Schönbach posits, for instance, that the accent in this work is on *innere Ergriffenheit* [inner emotion] (1894, 452), and Wapnewski speaks of an intensification/deepening of the literary traditions by Hartmann (1962, 96).

One of the enduring assumptions in interpretations of this work is that Heinrich's initial worldly existence, though perhaps not flawed on its own terms, is nevertheless faulty within some other moral or spiritual framework. Schönbach (1894) observed that Heinrich inappropriately saw his initial good fortune as the result of his own merit and not as coming from God, an idea that was to underlie many subsequent interpretations. For Sparnaay the main theme of the work is visible in the initial episode: Heinrich's faultiness is seen in terms of self-aggrandizement, or *superbia* (1938, 11 and 15). Taking a highly critical position with respect to Heinrich's worldly accomplishments, Ohly argues that Heinrich's leprosy is the expression of an empty, fragile noble society that is alienated from God and deeply pathological (1958, 143). Wapnewski has expressed the view that Hartmann's critique of worldly, secular values in this work is more relentless than in *Gregorius:* "as opposed to *Erec, Iwein,* and *Gregorius,* this work is not about a hero who fails in the courtly world, but about the courtly world failing in the hero!" (1962, 102). Proponents of similar views have been Schirokauer (1951/52a, 263) and Nagel (1952, 40), with the latter stating that Heinrich's orientation to knighthood is a kind of idolatry. Appraisals such as these, that find sinfulness in Heinrich's initial worldly existence and posit that this existence has to be overcome or rejected — rather than merely placed in proper perspective — see a more strictly dualistic conception at the heart of the work. Sparnaay states, for example, that the work is pervaded by *Weltverneinung* (rejection of the world) and Augustinian dualism (1938, 111).

In the sixties scholars began to take issue with the more or less explicitly dualistic orientation in previous criticism. Cormeau considers that Heinrich's initial existence is not sinful in itself but that he is blind insofar as he believes his good fortune will be lasting (1966, 129). One cannot, according to Cormeau, begin to speak of sin until Heinrich refuses to accept the illness as God's will by attempting to achieve a cure (and by accepting the girl's sacrifice). Endres also adopts a more favorable position with respect to Heinrich's initial worldly existence by suggesting that the illness is not even really a punishment, but rather a sign that God has taken an interest in Heinrich's salvation (1967, 282). The debate on this point is ongoing: Duckworth (1990) has lent support to the thesis of Heinrich's initial sinfulness. Basing his argument on similarities he sees to passages in *Gregorius,* on the theology of figures such as Bernard of Clairvaux, William of St. Thierry, Bede, and Hrabanus Maurus, and on secular authors such as Freidank and Thomasîn von Zerclaere, Duckworth finds Heinrich guilty of "the love of honour, pride and vainglory" (78), but he avoids a strictly dualistic position: "An outright rejection of the world is not essential, but perseverance in God's service most certainly is" (79). Dahlgrün, on the other hand, is more sympathetic to Heinrich, stating that he not guilty of a conscious sin or of *superbia,* but rather of a *Fehlhaltung* (faulty orientation) that will last until his change of heart at Salerno (1991, 181). Correspondingly, the author Hartmann does not wish to condemn the courtly world, but only to criticize its "secular orientation" (213).

The role played by the young maiden in the work has long fascinated translators and scholars alike. The early appraisals were almost universally positive and generally more strictly secular in kind. For early readers this work was basically a love story that derived its power from the nameless maiden's seemingly selfless affection for Heinrich. Gervinus has a great deal of praise for the manner in which

Hartmann has portrayed the girl's unselfish devotion, calling it nothing less that miraculous (1853, 368). Vilmar's words in 1866 on the girl in his literary history are exemplary: "It will never again be possible to portray the pure, completely selfless love of a deep and pure feminine heart so appropriately and truly" (cited from Rautenberg 1985, 81). With increasing recognition of the complexity of this work came a variety of different appraisals of the girl and her desire for self-sacrifice, many of them not nearly as flattering as that of Vilmar. Sparnaay (1938) and Schirokauer (1951/2b) posited that the girl is based on the model of the medieval martyr saint and that her importance consisted exclusively in the role she plays for Heinrich's salvation. A view with different implications began to be articulated later in the 1950s: rather than viewing her solely in terms of her symbolic value for Heinrich, critics began to see the maiden as Heinrich's foil. Just as he is deficient in his all too worldly orientation, so too is she deficient in her one-sided orientation toward the beyond and in her depreciation of this world, which is a necessary and positive part of God's creation. This approach to the significance of the maiden, which increases her importance in the story but also subjects her actions to greater critical scrutiny, was instigated primarily by the (perhaps inappropriately) absolute assurance on the part of the girl that her actions will achieve her salvation, and by the seemingly immature intensity of her reaction to Heinrich's decision in Salerno not to accept her sacrifice.

Among the first to have problems with the manner in which the maiden proposes to put herself beyond the toils of this worldly existence was Fechter (1955), who, pointing out the divine origin of the world that the girl maligns in her speeches to her parents, makes the maiden herself responsible for her breakdown subsequent to Heinrich's refusal to accept her sacrifice. Willson (1958) goes as far as to accuse the maiden of *superbia* because of her inappropriate anticipation of God's providential action, while Buck (1964/65) finds the girl's exclusive orientation toward her own heavenly reward dubious. The more strictly psychological orientation of Wapnewski is more radical in its severity, suggesting that the girl is both fanatical and hysterical (1962, 101). It is clear that some of the more extreme versions of this line of interpretation present a view of the girl that is diametrically opposed to sentimental image of her of the previous century. Also critical of the maiden is the recent article of Smits, which draws attention to the manner in which her words about the troubles of marital life are undermined by Hartmann's representation of the girl's parents, who lead a pure and praiseworthy marital life before God (1989, 444).

While earlier interpretations such as that of Sparnaay, which unquestioningly accept as valid the girl's wish to sacrifice herself and the arguments she employs to achieve this end, posit a dualistic conception, the positions of Cormeau (1966) and Tobin (1973) express perhaps most succinctly a view of the maiden's significance that is consistent with a more gradualistic conception. Both of these critics argue that the girl *initially* represents a dualistic position that has to be modified in the direction of a more gradualistic conception of God and world and that one of the major goals of the work is to demonstrate such a modification. Cormeau also posits that the weakness of the girl's strongly dualistic arguments with her parents is demonstrated by the fact that the narrator Hartmann does not himself sanction them (1966, 30), a thought that has been influential, if not entirely uncontested, among later critics. Henne (1982) presents the final example in this survey of the critical scrutiny devoted to the maiden and her actions. Agreeing with previous critics that the girl's "speculation with respect to her heavenly reward" is problematical (Henne goes as far as to call it "unchristian," 197), Henne asserts that the maidens wish to sacrifice herself for Heinrich heretically usurps the place of God or Christ (198); his position is thus diametrically opposed to the idea that the maiden fulfills the function of Christ for Heinrich (this idea, represented by the earlier critics Schirokauer and Verweyen, is discussed below). The girl's motivations also demonstrate for Henne parallels to heretical gnostic-Manichean thought, which was based on a radical dualism (191). Pointing out that the girl seems to reconcile herself without difficulty to the happy worldly end of the work, which stands in stark contrast to her earlier rejection of the world, Könneker warns against one of the prominent tendencies of past criticism, which is to seek *Stimmigkeit* (consistency) in Hartmann's characterization of the maiden (1987, 77).

Nowhere is the debate between the advocates of dualistic and gradualistic conceptions more pronounced than in evaluations of Heinrich's change of heart and rejection of the girl's sacrifice in Salerno, which is perhaps the most crucial episode in Hartmann's work. The critical debate is starkest here because of the jarring proximity of the worldly/material and the religious/spiritual: it is the extraordinary beauty of the maiden's naked body, seen by Heinrich through a crack in the wall, that immediately brings about the change of heart (the *niuwe güete*) that symbolizes the beginning rectification of Heinrich's relationship to God. Two basic views, corresponding to the postulation either of a dualistic or of a gradualistic conception underlying the work, can be made out in the critical evaluations of this episode. The first, represented by Schirokauer (1951/52a and 1951/52b) and Verweyen (1970) among others, posits that the erotic element of the girl's nakedness is deemphasized if not rejected in favor of its spiritual significance. The girl's outer beauty is in this view merely an aspect of her symbolic, spiritual function for Heinrich: she symbolizes Christ bound on the cross (Verweyen, 77). This view is consistent with a deemphasis of the maiden's importance as such and focuses on her presumed spiritual function for Heinrich in contrast to her potentially erotic corporeality. In fact, both Schirokauer and Verweyen argue that the human body in its own right was not considered attractive in the Middle Ages.

Interpreting the girl's beauty solely as an aspect of her inner spiritual beauty has come under attack by many scholars who question the validity of applying rigorously religious standards to Hartmann's work, which, despite its strongly religious tone, clearly contains other genre elements. Pointing to the developing attachment between Heinrich and the maiden earlier in the work and to the happy ending, Seiffert (1963) and Cormeau (1966) have argued that the physical dimension of the girl's appearance in this episode cannot be rejected or ignored, that it is in fact entirely consistent with the narrative logic of Hartmann's tale. The physical aspect of the girl's beauty does not merely establish narrative continuities between the earlier attachment and the later marriage; within a gradualistic conception on the part of Hartmann, this physical element could serve as a means of linking the physical with its higher spiritual source. This kind of argument is made by Tobin (1973): "Seeing the physical beauty of the naked girl is the beginning of a spiritual conversion in the hero . . . the *maget* helps to bring about the spiritual conversion in Heinrich in a way completely opposed to her own thinking" (98). Other critics have stressed what they see as the overtly erotic character of this episode. A recent example of this is the article of Margetts (1988), which points out that this key episode "brings together a group of sexual metaphors: *mezzer* (verse 1209) is used as a phallic circumlocution; *wetzestein* (verse 1218) is used for the clitoris; *ane strîchen* (verse 1219) is used as a metaphor for deflowering and/or impregnation; *wetzen* (verse 1221) is a metaphor for copulation" (202). All of these meanings, according to Margetts, belong to popular traditions that are indirectly accessible in dialect dictionaries and other literary works (202). Positing that Hartmann has imbued this scene with a strongly sexual/erotic aura, which is perhaps linked to the girl's peasant background, Margetts argues that these metaphors — assuming they are not employed unconsciously or gratuitously — express for Heinrich and the maiden "the erotic sexual aspect of their togetherness" (208–9). The recent article of Wailes (1992) posits the theme of incest as a subtext in *Der arme Heinrich,* perhaps as a covert continuation of the concerns developed in Hartmann's previous work, *Gregorius.* The covert theme of incest becomes manifest in the episode in Salerno, which involves the relationship of a child (*kint*) to an older man with whom she has developed an erotic bond. In the view of Wailes, Heinrich's change of heart involves the substitution of a covert, implicitly incestuous kind of father-child relationship with a relationship in which Heinrich can understand his feelings for the girl as those of a man for a woman (78).

All of the interpretations — from the covertly to the explicitly erotic — which focus on the corporal beauty of the maiden as having some value in and of itself — clearly undermine the idea of a consistently dualistic conception in *Der arme Heinrich,* and are perhaps more consistent with a gradualistic conception of the work that posits a movement from the initial worldly orientation of Heinrich and the initial spiritual orientation of the girl toward a middle position that rejects neither worldliness (even in its erotic corporeality) nor spirituality, but rather establishes an appropriate (i.e., for Hartmann and his audience) balance between the two orientations. It is the establishment of this balance that may be manifested in the Salerno episode. Although he does not linger on the value of the girl's physical beauty, Jackson also offers an interpretation that is consistent with a gradualistic conception, speaking of an inner moral breakthrough on the part of Heinrich (1994, 200); in *Der arme Heinrich,* according to Jackson, Hartmann explores "an inner, moral world which had previously been the province of the Church" (201).

The happy ending of the story has drawn critical attention primarily because of the jarring political and social mismatch that the marriage between Heinrich and the peasant maiden represents. According to Könneker, there is universal recognition that such a marriage is contrary to legal and social practice in the High Middle Ages, and even to the manner in which marriage was portrayed in literature, where the social equality of the partners was the most important criterion (1987, 81). Prominent among explanations of this problematical end is the thesis that the marriage of Heinrich and the maiden is the poetic reworking of the historical marriage of one of Hartmann's own ancestors with a woman of lesser social standing. The idealized manner of its portrayal in Hartmann's work can thus be understood as poetic compensation for a historical marriage alliance that would certainly have had damaging effects on the social status of Hartmann's family or that of his patron(s). As attractive as such an interpretation may be — in providing the rare possibility of a link between one of Hartmann's works and concrete events in the life of its author — it is ultimately unprovable on the basis of evidence now available. Other critics have seen the ending as consistent with the narrative logic of a genre that is seen by some to underlie Hartmann's entire work: the fairy tale (de Boor 1953, 79). The ease with which this view can be put forward has led many critics (Könneker 1987, 81) to posit that it ignores rather than explains the problem. The 1979 essay of Borck focuses on words spoken by Heinrich in justification of his immanent marriage to the maiden: "Nû ist si vrî als ich dâ bin" (Now she is free just as I am). Borck argues that such a passage cannot be understood literally — as the daughter of a peasant in Heinrich's territory, the girl cannot be legally free in the same ways as the noble Heinrich — but rather figuratively. It is a spiritual and not a legal equality of birth to which Heinrich refers here, and such a spiritual equality of birth can be based on Corinthians 3,17. Borck concludes that Hartmann's aim with this ending is to question birth as the determining factor of nobility (48).

This cursory survey of interpretations indicates that criticism of *Der arme Heinrich* has moved from a more strictly dualistic conception of the work, in which the initial worldly existence of the hero is condemned or rejected, to a gradualistic conception, in which worldly interests and values do not relinquish their own validity (this movement corresponds to a similar shift in emphasis that is observable in *Gregorius* criticism). The preponderance in recent years of interpretations that stress the gradualistic tone of *Der arme Heinrich,* its accepting inclusion of both worldly and spiritual elements, suggests that critics are no longer comfortable with the view of this work as a kind of theological text that would be more at home among monks rather than among a lay noble audience. A gradualistic understanding of the work situates it in the religiosity of its time and allows it at the same time to be more open-ended with respect to its meaning(s) and genre allegiances. Moreover, a gradualistic conception implicitly questions the division that is sometimes made between Hartmann's presumably worldly works (*Erec, Iwein*) and his spiritual, legendary ones (*Gregorius, Der arme Heinrich*) and, beyond this, a view of the author's literary and possibly personal development (i.e., the spiritual crisis) that is shored up by this division. The logic of the gradualistic approach to *Der arme Heinrich,* while it may make it somewhat more difficult for us to perceive a profound psychological or spiritual crisis on the part of the author, makes it somewhat easier for us to view *Der arme Heinrich* as a work that was written for the same audience that could also enjoy works such as *Erec* and *Iwein*.

7: *Iwein*

With *Iwein*, which is generally seen as Hartmann's final work, the author returns to the world of King Arthur. This work has been praised by medieval and modern critics alike above all on the basis of the formal and stylistic excellence of Hartmann's poetic language. It was quite probably this work that was foremost in Gottfried von Straßburg's mind when he praised Hartmann's *kristallinen wortelîn* [crystal words], and most modern readers of *Iwein* have concurred with Gottfried's assessment. In contrast to the presumably earlier *Erec*, this work exists in many manuscripts (the introduction to McConeghy's 1984 English translation of the work cites fifteen complete manuscripts, and seventeen fragments; of these A and B have figured most prominently in critical editions), which is an indication of its great popularity among medieval audiences. The different versions of the story contained in these manuscripts has, paradoxically, made it difficult to reconstruct Hartmann's original work, although it is likely that standard editions reflect a version of Hartmann's tale that would have been recognizable as such to German audiences at the beginning of the thirteenth century. Despite the praise heaped upon it and the relative reliability of standard editions, *Iwein* has not enjoyed a great deal of attention from modern critics in comparison to Hartmann's other works (Cormeau and Störmer 1985, 27), but the increasing number of articles and books dealing with this work in recent decades indicates that this relative neglect belongs to the past.

The popularity of *Iwein* among medieval audiences is further evidenced by allusions to it in the works of later medieval authors, such as Wolfram von Eschenbach, Heinrich von dem Türlîn, Der Pleier, and Rudolf von Ems, and by visual representations of scenes from the work in the frescoes at Castle Rodeneck from the beginning of the thirteenth century (depicting Iwein's initial adventure at the fountain), which were discovered in 1972, and on the walls of the drinking room in the Hessenhof in Schmalkalden from around the middle of the thirteenth century (depicting the initial adventure and scenes from Iwein's wedding). Two scenes (of Iwein's battle against Ascalon and of his introduction to Laudine) were also woven into a tapestry produced in the first half of the fourteenth century which is now in the Freiburg Augustinermuseum. The general theme of the images contained in this tapestry is the enslavement of men to love. Notable in these iconographic depictions is the choice of Iwein's first adventure at the fountain and the manner in which this adventure has been isolated from its narrative context and taken on a value of its own (independent, for example, from the question of the hero's development). Thus, an episode, which in the narrative context of Hartmann's work is supposed by many (e.g., Wapnewski 1962 and Cramer 1966, which are discussed below) to be demonstrative of the hero's flawed condition, is visually depicted as an exemplary knightly battle on the part of Iwein. The implications of the uses to which visual images of episodes from *Iwein* were put for interpretation of Hartmann's work are still not clear (the article of Ott and Walliczek 1979 provides a recent overview of the critical discussion), but these images clearly suggest that Iwein's initial adventure was not always viewed as a transgression (a situation that would be consistent with the interpretations of Voß 1983 and Fischer 1983, which are discussed below). Based on similarities in their visual representation, Wells (1982) has considered the possibility of a relationship of iconographic tradition between depictions of Iwein's madness and the dream of Nebuchadnezzar in Daniel IV.

There were numerous versions of the Iwein story (the story "Owen and Luned" in the *Mabinogion*, the Old Norse *Ivens Saga*, the Swedish *Ivan, the Knight of the Lion*, Ulrich Füetrer's *Iban*, and the Middle English *Ywain and Gawain*), but it is clear that Hartmann's work is a close reworking of the version of Chrétien de Troyes, whom he follows much more faithfully than was the case with his earlier *Erec* (for which sources other than Chrétien have been frequently posited). The basic material that is shaped in all of these works is of Celtic origin, and a study of the manner in which this material may have evolved over the centuries is provided by Sparnaay (1938). At the beginning of the oral and literary traditions is the historical Owen, son of Uriens, who lived in the sixth century in north England. Owen is mentioned in the Welsh Gododdin cycle (from around 600), the *Historia Britonum* (History of the Britons; written around 829 and attributed to a priest of South Wales named Nennius), by Geoffrey of Monmouth in his *Historia Regum Britanniae* (History of the British Kings) from the first half of the twelfth century, and in the book of Taliesin (compiled in the fourteenth century but containing much older material). The development of the literary Iwein was basically the same as that of Erec and Tristan: an initial oral tradition involving the hero grew by epic enlargement as new episodes were added onto the original core story. Sparnaay posits three significant phases in the development of the Iwein material in the century preceding Hartmann's version. Given the importance of mythical motifs in Hartmann's work (which is also the focal point of Ó Riain-Raedel 1978), it is worthwhile to consider the phases posited by Sparnaay.

The first stage would have been an Anglo-Norman tale composed by a bilingual Breton around 1125 in South Wales, dealing with a fairy who appears one day at the court of a famous hero. In the name of her sister, who is the princess of a fairy realm, this fairy asks the hero in a song to accompany her back to the land of the fairy queen. Although the journey will be full of danger, the land itself is of exquisite beauty and the fairy queen will reward the hero with her love. The hero, skeptical about the request, sends a servant (cf. the later figure of Kalogrenant), who is not, however, deemed worthy to enter the fairy realm and has to return. The messenger appears again at the hero's court and sings an even more beautiful song about the beauty of her realm and of her princess. This time the hero departs with her; they cross over a body of water and come to a beautiful land where the hero sees great trees with unknown fruits. The wonderful song of the birds enchants his ear. There the fairy queen awaits in a beautiful garden, where the hero remains only for a short time before returning home. Soon however he becomes sick with longing for the fairy queen (cf. Iwein's insanity). She sends her messenger again, who heals the hero with a magic salve (cf. the healing of Iwein), then leads him back to the fairy realm. The central theme of this tale is the perilous journey of a mortal to the Otherworld, a prevalent theme in the preserved Celtic tales (Sparnaay 1938, 19).

Around 1150 an Anglo-Norman poet, one of the storytellers who presumably brought the insular Arthurian material to the continent, transformed this tale by adding other mythical motifs with which he was familiar (e.g., the fountain and the figure of the watchman [cf. Ascalon]), and thus arrived at the second stage in the development of the Iwein material. In this version the initial adventure at the fountain has approximately the same form it will have with Chrétien and Hartmann. Different is that the battle between Iwein and Gawein occurs upon the arrival of Arthur at the land of the fountain, rather than near the end of the work (this earlier occurrence of the battle is preserved in the *Mabinogion* version of the tale). Also, the reconciliation with his lady, brought about by the lady servant Lunete, follows almost immediately upon his healing by the lady with the magical salve. Although what is basically equivalent to the second part of the bipartite structure in the works of Chrétien and Hartmann has not yet been formed, it is notable that the tale has been linked at this stage to King Arthur (Sparnaay 1938, 23–25). The third stage is documented by the tale of Chrétien, who distances himself disdainfully from wandering storytellers, and by "Owen and Lunet" in the *Mabinogion*, with the French author effecting the most significant transformations of the material (31). Even if Sparnaay's view of the history of the Iwein material is a conjectural reconstruction based only on the preserved versions of the story, it sensitizes the reader both to the importance of the originally mythical material and to the manner in which a popular narrative tradition was being reshaped in the course of the twelfth century according to the tastes and interests of lay noble audiences. In his study of the mythical element in *Erec* and *Iwein*, Giesa (1987) combines Propp's analysis of the folk tale and Jungian archetypal psychology in arguing that the courtly works achieve an individuation of the hero that was not present in the original mythical material.

As a result of the close relationship of the German work to its French source, and of many other considerations that have little or nothing to do with medieval literature, *Iwein* has served throughout the nineteenth and into the current century as a kind of battleground between French and German literary scholars, who have endeavored to put forward either Chrétien or Hartmann as the superior author. At the beginning of this battle stood Lachmann who, in the foreword of the 1827 *Iwein* edition, wrote: "if we compare Hartmann's portrayal with that of Chrétien de Troyes and his English translators, there is no doubt that the German poet is far superior" (viii). The appraisal of Gärtner (1875) contains a notion that recurs in subsequent studies in an ideologically more neutral form, which is that Hartmann succeeded in imparting to the *Iwein* story a spiritual/psychological depth that his source work did not possess. Gärtner was able to explain the thought processes preceding Laudine's decision to accept Iwein as her husband, which were criticized by French critics and even by German critics such Barthel on the basis of its "artificiality" (61), in terms of an deep inner conflict that can be traced back to Hartmann's German *Gemüt* [cast of mind, disposition], which had to find unacceptable the superficial contours of Chrétien's Laudine characterization (50). Defending the work of the German author against attacks from critics such as Förster (1887), who had stated that Hartmann's version of *Iwein* represented an aesthetic development "downhill," Schönbach continued the praise of *Iwein* as a formal achievement: "Why shouldn't a more mature artist be in the position to appreciate better the potential in his sources and to transform the traditional material with a lighter albeit finer hand?" (1894, 457). Jeske praised the German author more generally on the basis of his ability to transform "the loose, episodic stories of his sources into well-conceived, coherent works of art" (1909, 121). In one of the less-impassioned appraisals from the German side, Drube asserts that most previous studies of Hartmann's relationship to Chrétien were interested in increasing the status of the former "at any price" (1931, 10). For Drube there is no doubt that the French author is superior to Hartmann in his creative faculties (101); on the other hand, Drube considers that it would be inappropriate to compare the two authors on the basis of formal criteria, on account of Hartmann's basically ethical orientation. A jarring attempt to define Hartmann's specific German-ness vis-à-vis Chrétien in the context of National Socialism is the interpretation of Halbach (1939), who, under the dedication to his parents, optimistically expresses faith in the Führer's knowledge that there is no hatred between the French and the Germans before undertaking to demonstrate, with reference to Hartmann's treatment of Chrétien, "wie deutscher Geist gewaltig sich anschickt, fremdes Gut nach seinem Bilde zu formen" [How the German spirit powerfully sets about to form foreign material in its own image] (11). A detailed analysis of the battle between French and German critics, which was rife with nationalistic commonplaces (e.g., the carefree Frenchman versus the deep and serious German) and frequently pursued with a thinly veiled ideological fanaticism, is contained in the recent study of Trimborn (1985).

Attempts to establish the uniqueness of Hartmann's work on the basis of the more didactic, courtly approach taken by the German author, and/or the greater spiritual/psychological depth of the German work, have in this century for the most part lost the strongly nationalistic tone of some of the early appraisals, although it might be argued that it remains difficult to this day to disentangle completely the discussion of Hartmann's language and style from these earlier battles between French and German critics. Sparnaay stresses the courtliness of the literary language of *Iwein,* which is especially striking when compared to that of *Erec,* which is much rougher and contains what is seen as uncourtly vocabulary (e.g., *maere* [story], *degen* [thane]) (1938, 80); a more courtly orientation is also visible to Sparnaay in Hartmann's endeavor to soften the figure of Laudine, which is undertaken in order to conceal the shortcomings of ladies (55). Wapnewski speaks of Hartmann's general tendency to move from the individual and the specific to the general, corresponding to what is typically seen as Hartmann's didactic or moralistic tendency, and of the greater stress the German author places on "Ebnung, Dämpfung und Glättung" [evening, softening, and smoothing], corresponding to Hartmann's more courtly orientation (1962, 61). In his comparison of narrator remarks and commentaries in the Arthurian works of Chrétien and Hartmann, Kramer (1971) considers that Hartmann's more idealistic approach resulted in the elimination of much of the irony that was in his French source works. The study of Cormeau and Störmer offers a detailed description of the various ways in which these critics consider that Hartmann endeavored to soften Chrétien's harsher and more ironic treatment of the Laudine figure (1985, 199–200), prominent among which is the introduction of *minne* [love] as a motivating factor in Laudine's decision to marry Iwein, who has just killed her previous husband, Ascalon. A couple of recent evaluations indicate that the assessment of the relationship of Hartmann's version of the work to that of Chrétien remains unresolved, even if it is no longer discussed in the polemical and nationalistic tones of the previous century. Stressing the independence of the German author is McConeghy, who speaks in the introduction of his English translation of *Iwein* of a greater insight on the part of Hartmann into the "inner feelings of his characters" and a "psychological deepening" that is present in the German work (1984, xxviii). For McConeghy the word *translation* does not begin to capture the manner in which Hartmann deals with both of Chrétien's Arthurian works:

> Hartmann's versions of Chrétien's Arthurian romances hardly warrant the name of translation. With their various additions, omissions, explanations, authorial comments, and rearrangements they should be viewed as independent works in their own right. (xxvii)

Trimborn, on the other hand, remains highly critical of separating the German from the French work in this way and argues that differences between the two may be based on nothing more profound than differing stylistic inclinations (1985, 445). Despite Trimborn's arguments most scholars today consider that the idea of courtliness, which manifests itself in a more distant and restrained style and in ethical reflection about the proper course of action in a given situation that seems to deepen the inner life of characters, distinguishes Hartmann's work from that of Chrétien. It is this more courtly rendition of the Arthurian works — the so-called *adaptation courtoise* (cf. Huby 1974; Fourquet 1977) — that is typically seen as Hartmann's specific contribution.

Differences between *Iwein* and Hartmann's presumably earlier works are often employed both in appraisals of the former work in particular (as will be seen in the survey of interpretations below) and in more general assessments of the author's career in its entirety. *Iwein* is frequently seen as a sort of synthesis in which the more overtly worldly concerns of *Erec* are constructively joined with the spiritual concerns of the legendary works that presumably followed. Schönbach's study, which begins as a study of *Gregorius* and ends by viewing the prologue of this legend as the key for understanding all of Hartmann's works, posits an increasingly religious orientation in the literary activity that culminates in *Iwein* (1894, 467). Sparnaay's (1938) analysis goes in the same direction, positing that *Schuld* [guilt] and *Sühne* [penance] are the theme of Hartmann's later Arthurian work. This spiritual dimension distinguishes *Iwein,* as an *Entwicklungsroman* [a romance of development] from the earlier *Erec,* in which the hero only reaffirms his initial ideal condition without moving as an individual beyond it (72). Other interpretations have taken a more purely secular approach to *Iwein;* for example, *Iwein* is frequently seen as a foil to the earlier *Erec*. Among the first to take this position was Scherer, who states that both of Hartmann's Arthurian works concern "the opposition between heroism and love, between devotion to knightly duty and the joys of tranquil domestic bliss" (1883, 182). In this century de Boor (1953) continues in the same vein: *Iwein* is not concerned with deeper spiritual matters; rather, it deals entirely with worldly matters and has to do with precisely the same problem that is treated in *Erec*, which is the proper relationship between the principles of *minne* [love] and *âventiure* [adventure], which de Boor sees in terms of marital responsibilities versus responsibility toward one's knightly peers. *Iwein* merely inverts the scenario of *Erec:* a single minded pursuit of adventure threatens the integrity of "the valid obligations of love" (81). In contrast to many earlier scholars and consistent with his completely secular view of this work as an answer to *Erec,* de Boor does not stress the German depth of characterization often posited elsewhere but considers instead that Hartmann's posture is nowhere more detached: "the impersonal coolness of the classical is characteristic of Iwein. Indeed, no work of Hartmann was written with a stronger attitude of detachment" (80). In this view *Iwein* does not build upon the legendary works presumably preceding it, but rather distances itself from these and returns to worldly concerns of his presumably earliest works. Such a view places in question the idea of a gradual progression in Hartmann's career from worldly to spiritual concerns and is more consistent with the idea that the order, and possibly also the treatment, of Hartmann's works was dictated by the demands of his patron(s), which makes it somewhat more difficult to view them primarily in terms of an increasingly depth, maturity, and/or spirituality on the part of the author (this point is discussed by Cormeau and Störmer 1985, 27).

As in *Erec* criticism, one observes in early appraisals of *Iwein* an inability to perceive a coherent narrative plan or structure. Although he praised this work for its "graceful style" and its "beautiful proportion" (1854, 61), Barthel otherwise presents a view of this work that is consistent with his view of *Erec:*

> the content contains much that is unpleasant. A series of the strangest adventures, which for the most part lack correspondence to one another, the lack of psychological motivation, . . . a complete weakness in truly artistic invention. (61)

Like Barthel, Gärtner was disturbed by what he perceived to be insufficient psychological (Gärtner uses the word *seelisch*) motivation (1875, 50). Goedeke implies a similar lack of a coherent structure when he describes Iwein's adventures as follows: "Wandering around, he frees a lion from a dragon and comes after all kinds of Welsh adventures back to Laudine, who reconciles herself with him" (1884, 92).

An interpretation that moved beyond the anachronistic search for plausible psychological motivation was not yet achieved by Sparnaay, according to whom the lion, which Hartmann took from Chrétien's tale "probably without any deeper motivation" (1938, 39), was employed solely as a means to stimulate the interest of the medieval audiences (later critics consider that the lion possesses an important *symbolic* function).

The search for compelling psychological motivation — rather than for symbolic correspondences — was one of the factors that prevented early critics from perceiving any deeper connection between the hero's development and the structure of the work, even as some recognized that *development* could probably not be understood the same way during the Middle Ages as it is by the modern critic. An example is provided by Gärtner (1875), who had to reconcile his major thesis that Hartmann achieves a greater depth of characterization (i.e., than Chrétien), with a recognition that this greater depth was not achieved according to the kind of consistent linear development that is pleasing to the aesthetic tastes of the modern reader (50). Interestingly, there is an early recognition of a nonlinear kind of progression in the Middle Ages. Gärtner cites a passage from an 1833 lecture by Lachmann concerning the conceptualization of development in the Middle Ages, which is worthy of citation here, since it describes a dynamic similar to that seen in the later conception of structure based on Christian typology:

> An ordered story, the planned development of events, appears as late as the twelfth century not to have been the task of the epic poet; the individual event was simply put forth and its circumstances described only to the extent necessary, and a new event brought about not by progression but rather by a jump. (50)

Although recognized early, this specifically medieval dynamic (which is also recognized in Saran's analysis of the songs [1889]) often seemed more an impediment than an aid to understanding, to the extent that critics continued to base their appraisals on linear progression and psychological coherence. Only later, when this dynamic began to be defined in terms of Christian typology (the "jump" to which Lachmann refers corresponding to the disjunction between the first and second segments of the bipartite structure), did it become more concretely productive for interpretation.

It is generally assumed today that *Iwein,* just as *Erec,* manifests the bipartite structure characteristic of all the so-called classical Arthurian works (those of Chrétien, Hartmann, and Wolfram von Eschenbach's *Parzival*). In the first structural segment, the hero responds successfully to a provocation (Kalogrenant's defeat at the hands of Ascalon) posed to him personally — as a relative of Kalogrenant — and to Arthurian knighthood as a whole, winning for himself a wife, a land and, perhaps most important, the honor of the Arthurian court upon his defeat of Kay. A crisis follows that roughly corresponds to Erec's *verligen* at his home castle of Karnant: Iwein misses Laudine's deadline, is upbraided by Lunete, and lapses into insanity. The second structural segment ensues in which, according to McConeghy (1984), "the hero regains his lost status by atoning for his earlier error and demonstrating those attributes that make him a worthy lord and husband" (xxx). In the foreword to his translation of the work (1979), Thomas, pointing to the dramatic character of the work (over half of it is direct discourse), suggests that the work, with its incongruity and occasional triviality, "resembles a modern comedy" and might be divided into a five-act play: the first act — to the end of Kalogrenant's tale — setting forth the basic theme, the second recounting the rise and fall of Iwein on the basis of the same "inordinate thirst for fame" that led to Kalogrenant's ignominious defeat, the third the fall into the animal state of madness and return to sanity that culminates in Iwein's pursuit and capture of the count of Aliers (a variation, or inversion, of Iwein's deadly pursuit of Ascalon in the previous "act"), the fourth the hero's gradual development from an obsession with honor to an attitude of *rehtiu güete* [just goodness] in the adventures culminating in the battle with Gawein (this "act" also repeats and varies many of the features visible in the earlier ones — Laudine is again reluctant to see Iwein [i.e., the knight with the lion] leave her land after he has saved Lunete in the trial by combat), and the fifth Iwein's return to Laudine's land and the reconciliation (which mirrors "act 2"). An emphasis of the dramatic is also visible in the study of Schröder (1972), who points at the recurrence of certain kinds of scenes in both *Erec* and *Iwein* that in his view would have shaped the audience's reception of the latter work (213–68). These two examples indicate the same situation that was observed in *Erec* scholarship: conceptions of structure range from the more purely "objective" classical bipartite structure, which is not so much grounded in specific events at the plot level as in a symbolic mode of thinking according to which an initial effort, however apparently ideal, is nonetheless merely a prefiguration of a subsequent effort, or fulfillment, that achieves true ideality and coherence of identity, to plot-oriented approaches to structure such as that of Thomas, which establish more-concrete connections between the posited structure and specific events in the story but perhaps pay the price of seeming to be a somewhat more arbitrary ordering of events by the modern critic.

As was the case with *Erec,* interpretations of *Iwein*'s plot focusing on development have oscillated between a religious and a more secular, courtly view of the work, and because of the discussed tendency to view *Iwein* as a synthesis of the worldly and spiritual concerns of Hartmann's previous works, it is even more difficult to distinguish between them. Critics have also explored the exact role played by the overtly mythical elements that are just below the surface of the work. These elements are stressed in the appraisal of Kuhn (1953), which, much like Sparnaay's earlier analysis, sees in this work a dynamic of *Schuld* [guilt] and *Sühne* [penance]. Like Sparnaay, Kuhn stresses the fairy-tale elements in *Iwein,* arguing that they represent a consistent continuation of Hartmann's involvement with the more fantastic, legendary material that is treated in Hartmann's presumably previous work, *Der arme Heinrich* (83–84).

The interpretation of Wapnewski (1962) is based on the assumption that the transposition of the mythical materials into the courtly sphere went hand in hand with a moralistic intention on the part of the work's author. Wapnewski does not believe that Iwein's missing of Laudine's deadline is significant enough to motivate his adventures of atonement, asserting instead that the hero has brought more profound guilt upon himself by transgressing against the ideals of *triuwe* [loyalty] and *erbärmde* [mercifulness] in his killing of Ascalon (69). Although Hartmann does not explicitly call this a transgression (the words *âne zuht,* used in support of this interpretation, are ambiguous), Wapnewski considers his interpretation buttressed by the orientation of the second cycle of adventures (after Iwein's insanity) toward the good of others. This stands, for Wapnewski, in stark contrast to the goal of self-aggrandizement in the initial adventure that resulted in Ascalon's death (69–70).

Pointing to the small amount of scholarly interest garnered by *Iwein* in comparison to Hartmann's other works, Ruh (1965) was still involved in laying some of the foundations for a comprehensive interpretation of this work. Ruh argues that there is no reason to doubt that Iwein's missing of the deadline is his actual guilt; nor is there any reason to believe that this transgression is only symptomatic of a deeper problem (414–15). Iwein's ability to deal with *Terminschwierigkeiten* (difficulty with deadlines) in the second part of the work, called "medieval pedagogy par excellence" (415), confirms for Ruh that this is Iwein's transgression. Ruh turns his attention particularly to a problem that has continued to occupy scholars to the present day, which is the relationship of court society to *minne* [love], which is embodied by Laudine, the most purely mythical figure of the work. The continuing relevance of this complex problem indicates that there are problems involved in regarding *Iwein* as an inverted *Erec:* whereas Erec could regain his lost status merely by resuming the adventuring activity that he had neglected and by integrating his relationship to Enite into a broader recognition of his various responsibilities, it is not immediately clear why or how the same kind of adventuring activity that gets Iwein into trouble to begin with can win back the love of his lady Laudine, who dwells in a magical land outside the realm of Arthur and whose standards are presumably other than Arthurian. Ruh solved this problem by positing that Laudine and her realm come to occupy a second narrative point of focus next to the court of Arthur. The principles represented by Arthur's court (social responsibility) and Laudine's realm (love), although they are not united spatially, are linked temporally in the dynamic of Iwein's adventure, according to which the same acts that gain status in the eyes of the former also lead to a reconciliation with the latter (422–23). The value of the Arthurian court thus seems to some extent relativized, although Ruh's interpretation clearly does not posit that Arthurian values are criticized or rejected, which will be a recurring thesis among many later scholars.

Cramer's *Iwein* analysis (1966) sides with Wapnewski against Ruh, arguing that Iwein's guilt could hardly consist in the violation of an arbitrarily set deadline, but rather that it has to be indicative of a deeper inner problem. This problem is traced by Cramer back to the killing of Ascalon: in contrast to the correct form of adventure, which involves subjecting oneself to unknown dangers, Iwein rides out to face Ascalon and eventually kills him in full knowledge of what lies before him. Cramer sees in this a violation of law, indicative of an underlying attitude of *superbia* (a similar assessment is offered by Thomas 1979, 10–11). Iwein's problem is overcome in the second part of the work, not in a transformation that occurs "as a gradual and increasingly profound internal betterment of the hero . . ." (436), but rather in adventures that, when compared with the faulty adventure at the fountain, indicate different priorities on the part of Iwein (e.g., Iwein, fighting for another [the lady of Narison] and not himself, pursues the count of Aliers across drawbridge, just as he once pursued Ascalon, but this time he does *not* kill the fleeing knight). Symbolic of Iwein's correct orientation is the lion, symbol of *Recht* [justice, right].

One of the more overtly religious interpretations is Wehrli's essay dealing with the significance of Iwein's fall into insanity, another topic that has stimulated the interest of scholars to the present day. Viewing the scene depicting Iwein's madness as a critical link between the first and second parts of the work, Wehrli (1969), who also feels that the violation of Laudine's deadline is merely symptomatic of a deeper problem, argues that Iwein's madness can be seen in terms of an alienation from self that is consistent with a Christian conception of the human condition traceable back to St. Augustine: "Man finds himself in a condition of alienation from himself and consequently of restless seeking — because he, as a sinful creature, can never be self-sufficient" (498). Iwein's madness is for Wehrli symbolic of a spiritual awakening, in which the sinful hero of the initial adventure dies and is reborn to a higher, truer existence. The lion symbolizes Christ, the model upon which this rebirth is ultimately based. Thus, at the core of this work is "an omnipresent principle of Christian-religious ethics" (501).

A sociohistorical interpretation of Hartmann's Arthurian works, influenced by the Marxist-oriented studies of Erich Köhler, was put forward by Kaiser (1973). Kaiser viewed *Iwein* (just as *Erec*) as reflective of the interests and concerns of the *ministeriales,* functionaries at the larger courts whose unfree legal status did not correspond to the social status and considerable power they often wielded. Kaiser reads the Arthurian works as a sublimated wish on the part of this group, to which Hartmann and most of the courtly authors of his day belonged, to move up in the social hierarchy, just as Iwein seems to do by winning a queen and a land in his adventure by the fountain. The wish is however articulated according to the socially affirmative *Dienstethos* [service ethic] of the *ministeriales* that rejects unnecessary violence. Iwein acts in his initial adventure against this ethic, attempting to achieve "a rise in social position at any price," and in the second part of the work a proper orientation is achieved by Iwein in adventures that are performed in the service of others (119–20).

The study of Nölle (1974) is reminiscent of the earlier studies of Schönbach (1894) and Sparnaay (1938) in positing that Iwein, like the heroes of the previous legendary works, has to achieve a greater spiritual depth. Into the central thesis that Hartmann's work is more deeply religious than that of the playful Chrétien (7–8), Nölle incorporates another idea that has enjoyed widespread popularity among Iwein scholars, which is that Iwein's development takes him beyond the deficient standards of the Arthurian court to a higher and truer level of existence. In an exemplary *Entwicklungsgang* [development], Iwein eventually overcomes the standards of the *Scheinwelt* [illusory world] of Arthur, which are based on *Kampf* [battle] and *êre* [honor], and arrives at a deeper, more spiritual form of identity, for which the lion, "the visual expression of grace," is a sign (69). The greater spirituality achieved by Iwein is equivalent to a higher degree of individuality, according to the idea that individuality in the Middle Ages manifested itself primarily in spiritual or religious ways. With respect to formal artistry, Hartmann's greater emphasis of proportion, which according to Scholastic thought was the foundation of the beautiful (which was itself linked to the good and the true), gives formal expression to the same ideal to which Iwein aspires on the plot level (72).

The study of Lewis (1975) also supports the idea that Iwein's adventures eventually lead to a form of self-perfection that takes him beyond the form of knightly identity represented by King Arthur. For Lewis, Iwein's initial adventure — his killing of Ascalon — and his breaking of Laudine's deadline both reveal inner flaws that result from his adherence to deficient Arthurian ideals. Lewis does not view the problematic integration of the Laudine plot-line into the courtly world of Arthur in terms of the problematical reconciliation of different (mythic versus courtly) forms of narratives on a broader level, but rather as the result of a conscious choice on the part of Iwein to pursue his own knightly glory rather than to "accept his responsibility as Laudine's husband" (89). The battle with Gawein symbolizes both a physical and moral superiority of Iwein over the court of Arthur (101), and the final scene, which sees him reunited with Laudine, indicates that he has finally overcome the flawed Arthurian standards that guided his initial behavior.

Mertens's study of Laudine (1978b), which pursues a sociohistorical line of interpretation similar to that contained in his *Gregorius*-study of the same year, is based on the assumption that Laudine's concern for the integrity of her territorial and political authority would have offered a possibility for identification (*Identifikationsangebot*) to Hartmann's audiences. The killing of Ascalon and the subsequent marriage of Laudine and Iwein — undertaken by Laudine for political reasons — are not, according to Mertens, subjected to criticism. Instead, the problem is introduced by Iwein's missing of the deadline, the effect of which is again to place the integrity of Laudine's rule in doubt. Kraft's (1979) sociohistorically oriented study sees the adventures of Iwein primarily in terms of the value of *triuwe* [loyalty], which Kraft believes possesses a quasi-legal status and indicates at the same time the development of new kinds of interpersonal relationships based on Christian ideals. The overt problem — Iwein's neglect of Laudine's deadline — is indicative of an inner lack of *triuwe*, which is overcome in Iwein's adventures of atonement, in which this attitude is clearly manifested. Kraft considers that this interpretation is supported concretely by the plot and is critical of the attempt to seek the deeper meaning of the work in its structure. Zutt's study (1979), which is based on speech-act theory, focuses on the normative implications of language. In an analysis of a handful of key episodes, Zutt posits that the problem of the work is Iwein's failure to grasp the correspondence between words and actions that is necessary for normative action (71). Zutt's study thus reveals similarities to many articles dealing with the problem of language in Hartmann's *Erec* (Fisher 1986; Clark 1989; and Jacobson 1991). Kratins (1982) argues that Hartmann, in contrast to Chrétien, is concerned with the possibility of a divergence between the objective and the subjective. For Kratins, as for other critics (e.g., Nölle), the subjective is more or less equivalent to a religious standard, according to which "Iwein's natural chivalric self-assertiveness, his *Selbstherrlichkeit*, becomes nothing less than a spiritual liability" (213).

As he does in the case of *Erec,* Voß (1983) rejects the assumptions of studies positing an individual development on the part of Iwein, even where those studies (as in the case of Cramer 1966) profess to view such development in medieval and not modern terms. Attempting to go farther in the direction of objective guilt as discussed by Kuhn, Voß argues that guilt cannot be sought in the inner makeup of the hero, but rather in *transpersonalen Umständen* [transpersonal instances] (1). Positing an "unquestionably fixed homology between individual and collective value orientations" (see also Krause 1985, 234 and below) for the age of Hartmann (7), Voß questions the frequently articulated premise that Iwein ultimately transcends Arthurian values. Correspondingly, Iwein's adventure at the fountain is not seen as flawed in any way; rather, it is an exemplary instance of knighthood against a somewhat cowardly opponent. The fall of Iwein, just as that of Erec, cannot be linked to any specific deed at the plot level, where Iwein appears as exemplary in every respect, but rather is linked to the original sin of Adam and Eve. On a theological level Iwein is guilty in the Augustinian sense of original sin from the very beginning; as the representative of feudal-aristocratic values, Iwein remains flawless from beginning to end.

Fischer's (1983) study, a wholesale rejection of moralistically oriented interpretations (particularly that of Wapnewski 1962), gives striking testimony to the great variety of conflicting interpretations Hartmann's *Iwein* has been able to generate. Fischer evaluates *Iwein* as a work that reflects the increasingly secular values of court societies in the High Middle Ages, which are oriented primarily toward *sinnlichen Selbstgenuß* (*frutio sui*), the enjoyment of worldly things per se, independent from transcendental spiritual or moral principles (17). Fischer posits that attempts to entice a deeper religious or moral meaning from courtly works such as *Iwein* are doomed to failure (16–17) because they are not based on the works themselves, but rather on an anachronistic projection of modern moral categories that go in the direction of mistaking Hartmann for a medieval version of Immanuel Kant (61–66). Fischer believes Hartmann's work can be understood as it presents itself on the surface: Kalogrenant's definition of adventure, frequently criticized by modern critics, is entirely accurate (22); the battle against Ascalon wins an honor that is unquestioned in its value and constitutive of Iwein's identity (29–36); the problem that Iwein has to deal with is, as is stated in the work, the transgression of Laudine's deadline (96–98). Stressing the coincidence of objective and subjective in the Middle Ages in a manner similar to Voß but arriving at different conclusions on the basis of a self-reflective criticism of the philosophical premises underlying the assumptions of modern criticism, Fischer posits that the deeper moral meaning frequently sought in this work corresponds to the values of a bourgeois identity that would not come into existence until several centuries after Hartmann. A kind of analysis that is similar to Fischer's is contained in Czerwinski's 1989 study of *Erec*.

Articles by Schmitt and Krause (1985) have focused on Iwein's insanity in purely psychological terms, thus rejecting the idea that its primary significance is to be sought in Christian symbolism (cf. Wehrli 1969; discussed above). Schmitt points out that Iwein manifests symptoms that are, in early Scholastic medical treatises (e.g., the *De melancholia* of Constantinus Africanus), associated with the disease of melancholy, and he conjectures that Chrétien and Hartmann were familiar with the medical profile of this malady and perhaps even had firsthand experience with insane people (210–12). Krause sees Iwein's insanity from the perspective of a modern psychiatric school of thought that rejects physical explanations of insanity and looks instead at disturbances in interpersonal communication. In the case of Iwein, the disturbance is to be found in the conflicting demands of two communicative systems in which Iwein is involved, one connected to his service to King Arthur, the other to his status as ruler over the land of Laudine. As there is no individual identity outside these two systems that could stabilize their conflicting demands (and consequently no individual *Schuld* [231–32]; see also Voß above), insanity is a regression that is equivalent to "die beinahe vollständige Eliminierung der kulturellen Anteile des Verhaltens" [the almost complete elimination of the cultural components of behavior] (236). Graf's 1989 book on pathology in *Iwein*, which has the same kind of psychological orientation as those of Schmitt and Krause, defines Iwein's insanity, his *hirnsüchte*, as melancholy, which springs out of lovesickness. Going a step beyond Schmitt, Graf links Iwein's malady, which is described with precise medical terminology, to a programmatic conception of nobility (185). Instead of a process of guilt and atonement, we have, according to Graf, deviation (madness) and correction according to an aristocratic ideal of cultural progress that is projected upon the hero (191).

Other scholars have recently questioned the possibility of a single persuasive interpretation of Hartmann's *Iwein* because of the variety of different elements it contains. Two such essays focus on the figure of Laudine. Steiner (1985), pursuing her interest in the mythical component of the literary world of King Arthur that is more fully developed in her 1983 book on *Erec,* posits that the figure of Laudine — the purest embodiment of the mythical in *Iwein* — is never meaningfully integrated into the narrative. Whereas a meaningful development for Iwein can be observed, because he belongs to a (patriarchal) social order within which such a development can be measured, the mythical (matriarchal) remnants within Laudine ultimately prevent the court and its representative Iwein from establishing a meaningful relationship to her. This relationship remains *offen, unverbunden, ungelöst* (open, unconnected, unresolved) (248). Due to the mythical core within Laudine, this figure remains, according to the title of Steiner's essay, *unbeschreiblich weiblich* [indescribably feminine]. Steiner thus takes a figure (Laudine) and an element (the mythical) that many past critics have been at great pains to integrate into their interpretations (cf. Wapnewski 1962 and Ruh 1965; discussed above) and posits that such an integration is altogether absent.

Similarly, Ehrismann argues that the difficulty of understanding the figure of Laudine and its exact relationship to Iwein and his courtly world may be linked to modern expectations: "We have demanded rational causality where perhaps the acceptance of the non-causal could be constitutive" (1988, 92). Critical of a modern interpretive procedure that strives rationally and logically to integrate all elements of the work, even those that seem to resist such integration such as Laudine, Ehrismann suggests that a postmodern approach that is accepting of discontinuity and fragmentariness might more closely correspond to the historical constitution of a premodern work such as *Iwein:* "Im *Iwein* gibt es Ansätze gegen 'Einheitsobsession' und für 'Vielfalt' sowie für die Kunst des Umgangs mit ihnen — mehr nicht, aber dies immerhin" [in *Iwein* there are tendencies that work against unity obsession and for diversity and the art of dealing with it — nothing more, but at least there is this] (97).

Returning from the postmodern to the modern, I conclude this cursory survey of *Iwein* interpretations with a few recent studies that continue, and add depth to, the traditional idea that *Iwein* is to be understood within the broader moral/didactic inclinations of its author. Despite its somewhat unconventional preoccupation with the problem of mind — which focuses on the hero's mental state almost to the exclusion of everything else — Clark's 1989 analysis is in many respects reminiscent of past interpretations in positing that Iwein undergoes a developmental process in which he comes to the realization that he fights not merely to win, but rather to help others, and in which he also comes to understand what his obligations to his wife entail (168). Drawing attention to many differing critical approaches to *Iwein* (stressing contemporary legal norms, Christian virtues, feudal patterns of behavior, social responsibilities, etc.), which have resulted in the contradictory variety of *Iwein* scholarship today, Schnell (1991) argues in a recent article for the importance of a more subjective, ethical orientation on the part of Hartmann that is similar to that of Abelard. Hartmann, Schnell posits, wished to distinguish "between ethically relevant attitudes and the penally relevant result of an action" (15). One consequence of this position is to place in question other interpretations, such as that of Voß (1983), that stress the significance of objective instances. Kellermann (1992) turns her attention toward the prologue and the manner in which it is employed by Hartmann to "insinuate" the historical quality of his work. This historical quality — which enables the work to carry a moral significance — is seen by Kellermann as something that takes Hartmann far beyond his French source (16). Although familiar with the 1983 studies of Voß and Fischer (discussed above) and critical of the often simplistic way in which arguments positing individual development have been put forward in the past, Jackson (1994) nevertheless continues to advocate a developmental interpretation, positing that in *Iwein,* as in *Erec,* the hero's ethically oriented chivalry in the second cycle of adventures surpasses his more self-assertive and retributive use of force in the first. Although Iwein is by no means a murderer in the initial adventure, according to Jackson, the very form of Hartmann's (and Chrétien's) romance suggests a subtle ethical criticism of it (278).

It is instructive that *Iwein,* which is frequently considered the synthesis and culmination of Hartmann's literary efforts — the work that perhaps most perfectly expresses his individual personality and style — is also perhaps the most difficult work to interpret. This is indicated by the appraisals cited here (which are only a small sample), some of which are diametrically opposed in their assumptions and conclusions. The interpretive difficulties posed by *Iwein* are connected to a perceived incongruence between the constitution of the hero's identity and objective instances in the work (the court of King Arthur, the land of Laudine). This incongruence seems to elicit two basic responses, which result in a variety of interpretations that are distinct in their detail: one can interpret this incongruence in terms of a subjectivity that transcends these objective instances (i.e., Iwein reaches a level of perfection that takes him beyond the court of Arthur), which typically corresponds at another level to a depth of artistic conception and a formal/stylistic excellence (however it my be formulated in detail) that distinguishes Hartmann's work from its French source; or one can insist on the continuing validity of these objective instances, which would imply that the individual identity of Iwein remains fragmented (or, at any rate, not satisfactorily defined according to a coherent psychology) and which would imply at another level that the work is not conceptually coherent, at least not from a modern perspective, and perhaps also not so distinct from its source. Since the work itself provides no unambiguous support for either position, the decision about which response to make in the case of *Iwein* — and in the interpretation of *all* of Hartmann's works to the extent that *Iwein* is a representative synthesis — seems to be thrown back on the modern reader.

8: Conclusion: A Return to Points of Departure?

THE VARIETY OF interpretations cited in this book, although they are only a small sample, indicates that it may not be appropriate to locate the major significance of Hartmann's works in their frequently stressed moral or didactic element, despite its undeniable importance, or to force Hartmann entirely into the role of court pedagogue. The interpretations surveyed here suggest that the works occupy an indeterminate position with respect to *prodesse* and *delectare;* to deep emotional engagement and aloof detachment; to dualism and gradualism; to Celtic myth, Christian typology, the narrative designs of French and Latin sources, and Hartmann's own creativity; to a Christian concern for the welfare of the soul, the worldly interests of the lay nobility in Germany (such as the representation of power on a broad level, of the sublimated social/political ambitions of a particular group such as the *ministeriales,* and/or of the specific interests of a lord and patron), and the author's more strictly individual concerns.

It is possible to regard this indeterminate position stylistically as the result of a poetic temperament that does not express itself as forcefully as that of a Chrétien de Troyes or a Wolfram von Eschenbach; a consequence of this seems to be that Hartmann, however much he is praised, will be considered a second rate author, not on the same level as his brilliant and deeper predecessor and successor. Kuhn characterizes this tendency — which he himself endeavors to discredit — as follows:

> Hartmann was too courtly as a courtly singer and writer of epics, too religious in the works of his religious crisis. He articulates in each case the ideals, the spirit of the time too purely, too safely. One does not believe that he has personally struggled for them . . . (1953, 69–70)

Generally, this indeterminate position functions as a hermeneutical provocation that calls for critics to take one side or another on a given issue (e.g., the question of Hartmann's dependence on/independence from Chrétien; the significance of spiritual as opposed to worldly values in his works), the hope being that one or the other side in a given debate will eventually be demonstrated to be factually correct and/or consensus forming. Underlying this response to the apparently indeterminate position of Hartmann's works is a conception of literary criticism as a linear process leading from error to knowledge, in which error is frequently associated with subjective distortion and knowledge with objective truth.

The variety of differing and sometimes conflicting interpretations presented by Hartmann scholarship today suggests that another response needs to be considered: the indeterminate position of Hartmann's works might be acknowledged as a distinguishing accomplishment, rather than as a stylistic flaw or a hermeneutical challenge. In these works one observes, perhaps for the first time in German literature, a poetic language of great scope and versatility that bears the imprint of many different (and sometimes conflicting) concerns and interests, without ever being entirely in the service of any one of them. This response is compatible with a broader conception of literary criticism as a project that is constructively shaped (rather than distorted) by the different values, interests, and priorities of modern critics, to the extent that it does not insist on the closure of a single correct meaning, but allows for the possibility of "differing, and equally valid readings." (Clark 1989, 6). Rather than the logic of linear progression, the dynamic at the heart of this conception of literary criticism perhaps more closely resembles the uncertainty principle: the more precisely one aspect of Hartmann's works is known, the less precise becomes knowledge of the others. Instead of a process leading to some kind of closure, the "progress" of criticism from this perspective takes the form of an increasing diversification of critical points of view, which build on the successes of previous interpretations, and branch out from these in different directions.

An increasingly prominent subjective element in the interpretation of Hartmann's works, of which I spoke in the introduction, seems to indicate signs of such a movement in different directions. This subjectivity has manifested itself in a variety of different ways. There are critics who have continued to view the works of Hartmann as expressing some deeper, presumably timeless human qualities or values (a recent notable example is Clark's 1988 study of mind). Those interpretations, for example, which posit that the heroes attain a level of perfection that takes them beyond the court of Arthur in the Arthurian works and beyond worldly/courtly values in the more spiritually toned works might be considered as continuing the Hartmann criticism of the previous century, albeit without the strongly nationalistic tone, to the extent that they understand the perceived lack of correspondence between the heroes' identities and other objective instances in the works in terms of a subjectivity that is grounded more or less explicitly in a nineteenth-century notion of *Bildung*. This critical tendency would not, of course, be a *new* development, but rather a continuation of critical approaches that began among the late Romantics and were never completely submerged by the objective frames of reference developed in this century. There are critics who build upon one or the other of these objective frames of reference, but in such a way as to reveal that it has not been objective enough, that it has not succeeded in eliminating basically modern notions, but only in containing them and giving them a modern look: Voß's (1983) critique of the *Bildung* ideal underlying the critical employment of the typological structure pointed out by Kuhn is a case in point. An interpretation such as this, while still striving to view the works objectively (i.e., despite what he sees as its imprecise use in the past, Voß endeavors to employ the typological model in a more consistently objective way), might nevertheless be regarded as subjective to the extent that it reveals the ongoing significance in the act of interpretation of an instance such as *Bildung* that pertains more immediately to the context of modern critics than to the context in which Hartmann's works were produced (and also to the extent that it departs from an analysis of events at the plot level of the work, as does Voß's analysis). Other studies are more overtly subjective and in a more self-conscious manner (i.e, they reflect on the constituent elements of their subjectivity): Fischer's (1983) attack on moralism as something that pertains more immediately to the values of modern critics than to those of Hartmann's feudal-aristocratic audiences is simultaneously the criticism of a Kantian perspective from a Hegelian/Nietzschean one; Steiner's (1983) critique of the adventure as a process in which a patriarchal order defines and constitutes itself in the ongoing subjugation of a mythical matriarchy has a clearly modern interest which does not detract from the efficacy of the reading.

Although the studies mentioned above, and others that put forward some other kind of subjectivity (the postmodern subjectivity of Ehrismann's Laudine article [1988]), weigh little against the bulk of Hartmann interpretations, in which subjectivity (particularly that of the critic) still seems to be considered more a problem than an asset — when it is considered at all — they are perhaps representative of a more general tendency in recent decades to stress the significance of points of departure: those of Hartmann's heroes, who do not go out into the world as clean slates, but rather (knowingly or not) as knights and the sons of free nobles; that of the author Hartmann as the articulator of the ideals and interests of courtliness and knighthood that are shared by other poets and by his presumably lay noble audiences; those of critics and readers of Hartmann as members of their own academic, disciplinary, and theoretical communities. Whatever its ultimate effects may be on the establishment of a consensus about the significance of Hartmann's works that goes beyond generalizations, there seems to be an increasingly tangible tendency to posit, in a variety of different ways, that what one starts out with is as important as what one acquires along the way. Within the broader framework of this return to points of departure, the interpretation of Hartmann von Aue is perhaps discovering the extent to which it is not merely a critical discourse about adventure, but also a kind of adventure itself.

Works Consulted

Editions

Das Büchlein

1842. *Die Lieder und Büchlein und Der arme Heinrich*. Ed. Moriz Haupt. Leipzig: Weidmann.

1968. *Die Klage-Das (zweite) Büchlein*. Ed. Herta Zutt. Berlin: de Gruyter.

1972. *Das Klagebüchlein Hartmanns von Aue und das zweite Büchlein*. Ed. Ludwig Wolff. Munich: Fink.

1979. *Hartmann von Aue: Das Büchlein; nach den Vorarbeiten von Arno Schirokauer zu Ende geführt und herausgegeben von Petrus W. Tax*. Ed. Petrus W. Tax. Berlin: Schmidt.

The Lyrics

1758/1759. *Sammlung von Minnesingern aus dem schwäbischen Zeitpuncte, CXL Dichter enthaltend; durch Ruedger Manessen, weiland des Rathes der uralten Zyrich, aus der Handschrift der königlich-französischen Bibliothek herausgegeben*. Eds. Johann Jakob Bodmer and Johann Jakob Breitinger. Zurich: C. Orell.

1842. *Die Lieder und Büchlein und Der arme Heinrich*. Ed. Moriz Haupt. Leipzig: Weidmann.

1857. *Des Minnesangs Frühling*. Ed. Karl Lachmann and Moriz Haupt. Leipzig: Hirzel. Subsequently revised by Friedrich Vogt, Carl von Kraus, and in the thirty-seventh edition by Hugo Moser and Helmut Tervooren. 2 volumes. Stuttgart: Hirzel, 1987.

Erec

1839. *Erec: Eine Erzählung von Hartmann von Aue*. Ed. Moriz Haupt. Leipzig: Weidmann.

1939. *Hartmann von Aue: Erec.* Ed. Albert Leitzmann. Halle: Niemeyer. Subsequently revised by Ludwig Wolff and in the sixth edition by Christoph Cormeau and Kurt Gärtner. Tübingen: Niemeyer, 1985.

Gregorius

1838. *Gregorius: Eine Erzählung von Hartmann von Aue.* Ed. Karl Lachmann. Berlin: Reimer.

1882. *Gregorius von Hartmann von Aue.* Ed. Hermann Paul. Halle: Niemeyer. Subsequently revised by Albert Leitzmann, Ludwig Wolff, and most recently in the thirteenth edition by Burghart Wachinger. Tübingen: Niemeyer, 1984.

Der arme Heinrich

1784. *Sammlung deutscher Gedichte aus dem XII., XIII. und XIV. Jahrhundert.* Ed. Christoph Heinrich Myller. Volume 1. Berlin.

1815. *Der arme Heinrich von Hartmann von Aue* [with a modern German prose translation]. Ed. Jakob and Wilhelm Grimm. Berlin: Realschulbuchhandlung.

1842. *Die Lieder und Büchlein und Der arme Heinrich.* Ed. Moriz Haupt. Leipzig: Weidmann.

1882. *Der arme Heinrich von Hartmann von Aue.* Ed. Hermann Paul. Halle: Niemeyer. Subsequently revised by Albert Leitzmann, Ludwig Wolff, and in the fifteenth edition by Gesa Bonath. Tübingen: Niemeyer, 1984.

1913. *Der arme Heinrich: Überlieferung und Herstellung.* Ed. Erich Gierach. Heidelberg: Winter.

Iwein

1784. *Sammlung deutscher Gedichte aus dem XII., XIII. und XIV. Jahrhundert.* Ed. Christoph Heinrich Myller. Volume 2. Berlin.

1786/87. *Iwain, ein Heldengedicht vom Ritter Hartmann, erkläret, mit Vorberichten, Anmerkungen und einem Glossar versehen.* Ed. Karl Michaeler. 2 volumes. Vienna: Taubstummeninstituts-buchdrukerei.

1827. *Iwein der riter mit dem lewen getibtet von dem hern Hartmann dienstman ze Ouwe.* Ed. G. F. Benecke and Karl Lachmann. Berlin: Reimer, 1827. The seventh revised edition is by Ludwig Wolff. Berlin: de Gruyter, 1968.

Secondary works

1853. Gervinus, Georg G. *Geschichte der deutschen Dichtung.* Vol. 1. 4th ed. Leipzig: Engelmann.

1854. Barthel, Karl. *Leben und Dichten Hartmanns von Aue.* Berlin: Schindler.

1859. Pfeiffer, Franz. *Über Hartmann von Aue zum Erec.* Vienna: Jacob.

1869. Wilmanns, Wilhelm. "Zu Hartmanns von Aue Liedern und Büchlein." *Zeitschrift für deutsches Altertum* 14: 144–55.

1872. Heinzel, Richard. "Über die Lieder Hartmanns von Aue." *Zeitschrift für Deutsches Altertum* 15: 125–40.

1874. Schmid, Ludwig. *Des minnesängers Hartmann von Aue stand, heimat und geschlecht. Eine kritisch-historische Untersuchung von Dr. Ludwig Schmid . . . Mit einem Wappenbilde.* Tübingen: Fues.

1874. Schreyer, Hermann. *Untersuchungen über das Leben und die Dichtungen Hartmanns von Aue.* Naumburg: Sieling.

1875. Gärtner, Gustaf. *Der "Iwein" Hartmanns von Aue und der "Chevalier au lyon" des Crestien von Troies.* Breslau: Grass.

1879. Schultz, Alwin. *Das höfische Leben zur Zeit der Minnesänger.* Leipzig: Hirzel.

1882. Muth, Richard V. *Mittelhochdeutsche Metrik: Leitfaden zur einführung in die lectüre der classiker.* Vienna: Hölder.

1883. Scherer, Wilhelm. *Geschichte der deutschen Literatur.* Berlin: Knauer.

1884. Goedeke, Karl. *Grundrisz zur Geschichte der deutschen Dichtung aus den Quellen.* Vol. 1. 2d ed. Dresden: Ehlermann.

1884. Monsterberg-Mückenau, Silvius von. *Der Infinitiv in den Epen Hartmanns von Aue.* Breslau: Koebner. Reprinted 1977: New York: Olms.

1884. Selisch, Adolf. "Zur Textkritik von Hartmanns *Gregorius.*" *Zeitschrift für deutsche Philologie* 16: 257–306.

1885. Henrici, Emil. "Die Handschriften von Hartmanns *Iwein.*" *Zeitschrift für deutsche Philologie* 17: 385–438.

1887. Förster, Wendelin. Introduction. *Der Löwenritter (Yvain) von Christian von Troyes.* Ed. Wendelin Förster. Halle: Niemeyer.

1889. Saran, Franz. *Hartmann von Aue als Lyriker: eine literarhistorische Untersuchung.* Halle: Niemeyer.

1890. Wlislocki, Heinrich von. "Volkstümliches zum *Armen Heinrich.*" *Zeitschrift für deutsche Philologie* 23: 217–25.

1893. Kleiber, H. *Hartmanns von Aue Erec und seine altfranzösische Quelle*. Königsberg: Hartung.

1893. Zwierzina, Konrad. "Überlieferung und Kritik von Hartmanns *Gregorius*." *Zeitschrift für deutsches Altertum* 37: 129–217 and 356–416.

1894. Schönbach, Anton E. *Über Hartmann von Aue; drei bücher untersuchungen*. Graz: Leuschner.

1895. Hagen, Paul. "Zum *Erec*." *Zeitschrift für deutsche Philologie* 27: 463–74.

1896. Erdmann, Oskar. "Zur Textkritik von Hartmanns *Gregorius*." *Zeitschrift für deutsche Philologie* 28: 47–49.

1896. Martin, E. Review of *Über Hartmann von Aue; drei bücher untersuchungen*, by Anton E. Schönbach. *Zeitschrift für deutsches Altertum* 40: 47–50.

1896. Schroeder, Edward. "Allerlei Iweinkritik." *Zeitschrift für deutsches Altertum* 40: 225–45.

1896. Vos, Bert John. *The Diction and Rime-technic of Hartman von Aue*. New York: Lemcke.

1898. Kraus, Carl von. "Das sogenannte 2. Büchlein und Hartmanns Werke." *Festgabe Richard Heinzel*. Halle: Niemeyer. 111–72.

1898. Piquet, Felix. *Etude sur Hartmann d'Aue*. Paris: Leroux.

1898. Saran, Franz. *Über Hartmann von Aue: das sogenannte II. Büchlein*. Halle: n.p.

1898. Zwierzina, Konrad. "Beobachtungen zum Reimgebrauch Hartmanns und Wolframs." *Festgabe Richard Heinzel*. Halle: Niemeyer. 437–511.

1900. Machule, Paul. "Zur einleitung des *Gregorius* Hartmanns von Aue." *Zeitschrift für deutsche Philologie* 32: 192–212.

1900. Zwierzina, Konrad. "Mittelhochdeutsche Studien." *Zeitschrift für deutsches Altertum* 44: 1–116, 249–316, and 345–406.

1901. Firmery, Joseph L. *Notes critiques sur quelques traductions allemandes de poemes français au moyen age*. Paris: Fontemoing.

1901. Zwierzina, Konrad. "Mittelhochdeutsche Studien." *Zeitschrift für deutsches Altertum* 45: 19–100, 253–313, and 317–419.

1905. Bartels, Adolf. *Geschichte der Deutschen Literatur*. Vol. 1. Leipzig: Avenarius.

1905. Tardel, Hermann. *Der arme Heinrich in der neueren Dichtung*. Berlin: Duncker.

1909. Jeske, Georg Gustav August. *Die Kunst Hartmanns von Aue als Epiker, verglichen mit der seiner Nachahmer*. Greifswald: Kunike.

1911. Peetz, Helmut. *Der Monolog bei Hartmann von Aue.* Greifswald: Adler.

1912. Heyne, Wilhelm. *Die Technik der Darstellung lebender Wesen bei Hartmann von Aue.* Greifswald: Adler.

1913. Langer, Theodor B. *Der Dualismus in Weltanschauung und Sprache Hartmanns von Aue.* Greifswald: Adler.

1917. Gierach, Erich. "Untersuchungen zum Armen Heinrich." *Zeitschrift für deutsches Altertum* 55: 503–568.

1917. Rosenhagen, Gustav. "Zobel von Connelant." *Zeitschrift für deutsches Altertum* 55: 301–2.

1918. Naumann, Hans. "Zu Hartmanns *Erec.*" *Zeitschrift für deutsche Philologie* 47: 360–72.

1920. Sparnaay, Hendrik. "Zur Entwicklung der Gregorsage." *Neophilologus* 5: 21–32. Cited from 1973: "Das Ritterliche Element in der Gregorsage." *Hartmann von Aue.* Eds. Hugo Kuhn and Christoph Cormeau. 7–16.

1921. Schwietering, Julius. "Die Demutsformel mittelhochdeutscher Dichter." *J. Schw. Philologische Schriften.* Ed. Friedrich Ohly. Munich: Fink. 1969. 140–215.

1922. Bürck, Emma. *Sprachgebrauch und Reim in Hartmans Iwein.* Munich: Callway.

1922. Hauck, Albert. *Kirchengeschichte Deutschlands.* Leipzig: Hinrich.

1927. Ehrismann, Gustav. *Geschichte der deutschen Literatur bis zum Ausgang des Mittelalter.* Munich: Beck.

1929. Witte, A. "Hartmann von Aue und Kristian von Troyes." *Beiträge zur Geschichte der deutschen Sprache und Literatur* 53: 65–194.

1931. Drube, Herbert W. *Hartmann und Chretien.* Münster: Aschendorff.

1933. Jantzen, Hermann. *Hartmann von Aue und Gottfried von Straßburg: Eine Auswahl mit Anmerkungen und Wörterbuch.* 2d ed. Berlin: de Gruyter.

1933. Sparnaay, Hendrik. *Hartmann von Aue: Studien zu einer Biographie.* Vol. 1. Halle. (This and the 1938 volume of Sparnaay's Hartmann biography were reprinted in 1975 (Darmstadt: Wissenschaftliche Buchgesellschaft.)

1934. Fourquet, Jean. "Zobel aus Connelant." *Zeitschrift für deutsches Altertum* (71): 268.

1936. Kuhn, Hugo. "Mittelalterliche Kunst und ihre *Gegegebenheit.*" *Deutsche Vierteljahrschrift* 14: 223–45.

1937. Ittenbach, Max. *Deutsche Dichtungen der salischen Kaiserzeit und verwandte Denkmäler.* Würzburg-Aumühle: Triltsch.

1938. Sparnaay, Hendrik. *Hartmann von Aue: Studien zu einer Biographie*. Vol. 2. Halle. (This and the 1933 volume of Sparnaay's Hartmann biography were reprinted in 1975 (Darmstadt: Wissenschaftliche Buchgesellschaft.)

1939. Elias, Norbert. *Über den Prozeß der Zivilisation*. Vol. 2. Basel: Verlaghaus zum Falken.

1939. Halbach, Kurt. *Franzosentum und Deutschtum in höfischer Dichtung des Stauferzeitalters*. Berlin: Junker.

1942. Nordmeyer, Henry W. "Minnesangforschung und Psychologie." *Monatshefte* 34: 274–79.

1948. Kuhn, Hugo. "Erec." *Festschrift für Kluckhohn und Schneider*. Tübingen: Mohr. 122–50. Cited from 1973: *Hartmann von Aue*. Eds. Hugo Kuhn and Christoph Cormeau. 17–48.

1950. Schieb, Gabriele. "Schuld und Sühne in Hartmanns *Gregorius*." *Beiträge zur deutschen Sprache und Literatur* 72: 51–64.

1951/52a. Schirokauer, Arno. "Die Legende vom Armen Heinrich." *Germanisch Romanische Monatsschrift* 33: 262–68.

1951/52b. Schirokauer, Arno. "Zur Interpretation des Armen Heinrich." *Zeitschrift für deutsches Altertum* 83: 59–78.

1952. Nagel, Bert. *Der arme Heinrich Hartmanns von Aue: eine Interpretation*. Tübingen: Niemeyer.

1952. Sparnaay, Hendrik. "Zu Hartmanns Kreuzzugslyrik." *Deutsche Vierteljahrschrift* 26: 162–77.

1953. Boor, Helmut de. *Die höfische Literatur: Vorbereitung, Blüte, Ausklang 1170-1250*. Vol. 2. of *Geschichte der deutschen Literatur*. By Helmut de Boor and Richard Newald. Munich: Beck.

1953. Frenzel, Herbert A., and Elisabeth Frenzel. *Daten deutscher Dichtung: Chronologischer Abriß der deutschen Literaturgeschichte*. Cologne: Kiepenheuer. 21st ed. in 1984. Vol.1. Munich: Deutscher Taschenbuch Verlag.

1953. Kuhn, Hugo. "Hartmann von Aue als Dichter." *Der Deutschunterricht* 5: 11–27. Cited from 1973: *Hartmann von Aue*. Eds. Hugo Kuhn and Christoph Cormeau. 68–86.

1954. Zuntz, Günther. "*Ödipus und Gregorius*: Tragödie und Legende." *Antike und Abendland* 4: 191–203. Cited from 1973: *Hartmann von Aue*. Eds. Hugo Kuhn and Christoph Cormeau. 87–107.

1955. Fechter, Werner. "Über den *Armen Heinrich* Hartmanns von Aue." *Euphorion* 49: 1–28.

1956. Eggers, Hans. *Symmetrie und Proportion epischen Erzählens*. Stuttgart: Klett.

1956. Neumann, Friedrich. "Der *Arme Heinrich* in Hartmanns Werk." *Zeitschrift für deutsche Philologie* 75: 225–55.

1957. Nobel, Hildegard. "Schuld und Sühne in Hartmanns *Gregorius* und in der frühscholastischen Theologie." *Zeitschrft für deutsche Philologie* 76: 42–79.

1957. Schröder, Werner. "Zur Chronologie der drei großen mittelhochdeutschen Epiker." *Deutsche Vierteljahrschrift* 31: 264–302.

1958. Ohly, Walter. *Die heilsgeschichtliche Struktur der Epen Hartmanns von Aue*. Dissertation. Freie Universität Berlin.

1958. Willson, Harold B. "Symbol and Reality in *Der arme Heinrich*." *Modern Language Review* 53: 526–36.

1959a. Kuhn, Hugo. "Parzival. Ein Versuch über Mythos, Glaube und Dichtung im Mittelalter." *Dichtung und Welt im Mittelalter*. Stuttgart: Metzler. 151–180.

1959b. Kuhn, Hugo. "Soziale Realität und dichterische Fiktion am Beispiel der höfischen Ritterdichtung Deutschlands." *Dichtung und Welt im Mittelalter*. Stuttgart: Metzler. 22–40.

1959. Willson, Harold B. "Hartmann's *Gregorius* and the Parable of the Good Samaritan." *Modern Language Review* 54: 195–203.

1960. Gottfried von Straßburg. *Tristan*. Trans. A. T. Hatto. New York: Penguin Books.

1961. Fourquet, Jean. "Zum Aufbau des *Armen Heinrich*." *Wirkendes Wort* 11.3. Sonderheft. 12–24.

1961/62. Grosse, Siegfried. "Beginn und Ende der erzählenden Dichtungen Hartmanns von Aue." *Beiträge zur Geschichte der deutschen Sprache und Literatur* 83: 137–56. Cited from 1973: *Hartmann von Aue*. Eds. Hugo Kuhn and Christoph Cormeau. 172–94.

1962. Bennholdt-Thomsen, Anke. "Die allegorischen *kleit* im *Gregorius*-Prolog." *Euphorion* 56: 174–184. Cited from 1973: *Hartmann von Aue*. Eds. Hugo Kuhn and Christoph Cormeau. 195–216.

1962. Wapnewski, Peter. *Hartmann von Aue*. Stuttgart: Metzler. Seven editions by 1979.

1963. King, Kenneth C. "Zur Frage der Schuld in Hartmanns *Gregorius*." *Euphorion* 57: 44–66. Cited from 1973: *Hartmann von Aue*. Eds. Hugo Kuhn and Christoph Cormeau. 311–41.

1963. Seiffert, Leslie. "Das Herz der Jungfrau: Legende und Märchen im *Armen Heinrich*." *Deutsche Vierteljahrschrift* 37: 384–405. Cited from 1973: *Hartmann von Aue*. Eds. Hugo Kuhn and Christoph Cormeau. 254–86.

1963. Tax, Peter. "Studien zum Symbolischen in Hartmanns *Erec:* Erec's ritterliche Erhöhung." *Wirkendes Wort* 13: 277–88. Cited from 1973: *Hartmann von Aue.* Eds. Hugo Kuhn and Christoph Cormeau. 287–310.

1963. Wisniewski, Roswitha. "Hartmanns Klage-Büchlein." *Euphorion* 57: 341–369. Cited from 1973: *Hartmann von Aue.* Eds. Hugo Kuhn and Christoph Cormeau. 217–53.

1964/65. Buck, Timothy. "Hartmann's *Reine maget.*" *German Life and Letters* 18: 169–76.

1964. Jong, Jan de. *Hartmann von Aue als Moralist in seinen Artusepen.* Amsterdam: Soest.

1964. Kaiser, Erich. *Das Thema der unheilbaren Krankheit im 'Armen Heinrich' Hartmanns von Aue und im 'Engelhard' Konrads von Würzburg und weiteren mittelhochdeutschen Gedichten.* Ulm: Köhler.

1964. Schwarz, Werner. "Free will in Hartmann's *Gregorius.*" *Beiträge zur Geschichte der deutschen Sprache und Literatur* 89: 129–50. (Republished in 1984; cf. below.)

1964. Wolf, Alois. *Gregorius bei Hartmann von Aue und Thomas Mann.* Munich: Oldenbourg.

1965. Ruh, Kurt. "Zur Interpretation von Hartmanns *Iwein.*" *Philologia deutsch. Festschrift zum 70. Geburtstag von Walter Henzen.* Eds. Werner Kohlschmidt and Paul Zinsli. Bern: Francke. 39–51. Cited from 1973: *Hartmann von Aue.* Eds. Hugo Kuhn and Christoph Cormeau. 408–25.

1965. Schottmann, Hans. "*Gregorius* und *Grégoire.*" *Zeitschrift für deutsches Altertum und Literature* 94: 81–108. Cited from 1973: *Hartmann von Aue.* Eds. Hugo Kuhn and Christoph Cormeau. 373–407.

1965. Sparnaay, Hendrik. "Brauchen wir ein neues Hartmannbild?" *Deutsche Vierteljahrschrift* 39: 639–50.

1966. Cormeau, Christoph. *Hartmanns von Aue Armer Heinrich und Gregorius. Studien zur Interpretation mit dem Blick auf die Theologie zur Zeit Hartmanns.* Munich: Beck.

1966. Cramer, Thomas. "*Saelde und êre* in Hartmanns *Iwein.*" *Euphorion* 60: 30–47. Cited from 1973: *Hartmann von Aue.* Eds. Hugo Kuhn and Christoph Cormeau. 426–49.

1966. Dittmann, Wolfgang. *Hartmanns Gregorius: Untersuchungen zur Überlieferung, zum Aufbau und Gehalt.* Berlin: Schmidt.

1967. Endres, Rolf. "Heinrichs *hôchvart.*" *Euphorion* 61: 267–94.

1967. Ruh, Kurt. *Höfische Epik des deutschen Mittelalters.* Vol. 1. Berlin: Schmidt.

1968. Blattmann, Ekkehard. *Die Lieder Hartmanns von Aue*. Berlin: Schmidt.

1968. Klemt, Ingrid. *Hartmann von Aue: Eine Zusammenstellung der über ihn und sein Werk von 1927 bis 1965 erschienenen Literatur.* Köln: Greven.

1968. Kuhn, Hugo. "Minnesang als Aufführungsform." *Festschrift für K. Ziegler*. Eds. Eckehard Catholy and Winfried Hellmann. Niemeyer: Tübingen. 1–12. Cited from 1973: *Hartmann von Aue*. Eds. Hugo Kuhn and Christoph Cormeau. 478–90.

1968. Linke, Hansjürgen. *Epische Strukturen in der Dichtung Hartmanns von Aue; Untersuchungen zur Formkritik, Werkstruktur und Vortragsgliederung*. Munich: Fink.

1969. Wehrli, Max. "Iweins Erwachen." *Geschichte, Deutung, Kritik, Literaturwissenschaftliche Beiträge, dargebracht zum 65. Geburtstag Werner Kohlschmidts*. Eds. Maria Bindschedler and Paul Zinsli. Bern: Francke. 64–78. Cited from 1973: *Hartmann von Aue*. Eds. Hugo Kuhn and Christoph Cormeau. 491–510.

1970. Carne, Eva-Maria. *Die Frauengestalten bei Hartmann von Aue. Ihre Bedeutung im Aufbau und Gehalt der Epen*. Marburg: Elwert.

1970. Eroms, Hans-Werner. *Vreude bei Hartmann von Aue*. Munich: Fink.

1970. Köhler, Erich. "Vergleichende soziologische Betrachtungen zum romanischen und zum deutschen Minnesang." *Berliner Germanistentag*. Eds. Karl Heinz Borck and Rudolf Henss. Heidelberg: Winter. 63–76.

1970. Okken, Lambertus. *Ein Beitrag zur Entwirrung einer kontaminierten Manuskripttradition; Studien zur Überlieferung von Hartmanns von Aue Iwein*. Doctoral thesis. University of Utrecht.

1970. Verweyen, Theodor. *Der Arme Heinrich Hartmanns von Aue: Studien und Interpretation*. Munich: Fink.

1971. Kramer, Hans-Peter. *Erzählerbemerkungen und Erzählerkommentare in Chrestiens und Hartmanns Erec und Iwein*. Göppingen: Kümmerle.

1971. Seigfried, H. "Der Schuldbegriff im *Gregorius* und im *Armen Heinrich* Hartmanns von Aue." *Euphorion* 65: 162–82.

1972. Cramer, Thomas. "Soziale Motivation in der Schuld-Sühne Problematik von Hartmanns *Erec*." *Euphorion* 66: 97–112.

1972. Schröder, Joachim. *Zu Darstellung und Funktion der Schauplätze in den Artusromanen Hartmanns von Aue*. Göppingen: Kümmerle.

1973. Borst, Arno. *Lebensformen im Mittelalter*. Frankfurt a.M.: Ullstein.

1973. *Hartmann von Aue*. Eds. Hugo Kuhn and Christoph Cormeau. Darmstadt: Wissenschaftliche Buchgesellschaft.

1973. Heinze, Norbert. *Zur Gliederungstechnik Hartmanns von Aue; stilistische Untersuchungen als Beitrag zu einer strukturkritischen Methode*. Göppingen: Kümmerle.

1973. Kaiser, Gert. *Textauslegung und gesellschaftliche Selbstdeutung: Aspekte einer sozialgeschichtlichen Interpretation von Hartmanns Artusepen*. Frankfurt: Athenäum. A revised edition appeared in 1978. Wiesbaden: Akademische Verlagsgesellschaft.

1973. Peters, Ursula. "Niederes Rittertum oder hoher Adel? Zu Erich Köhlers historisch-kritischer Deutung der altprovenzalischen und mittelhochdeutschen Minnelyrik." *Euphorion* 67: 244–60.

1973. Tobin, Frank J. *Gregorius and Der arme Heinrich; Hartmann's dualistic and gradualistic views of reality*. Bern: Lang.

1974. Brody, Saul N. *The Disease of the Soul: Leprosy in Medieval Literature* (Ithaca: Cornell University Press).

1974. Goebel, K. Dieter. *Untersuchungen zu Aufbau und Schuldproblem in Hartmanns Gregorius*. Berlin: Schmidt.

1974. Gössmann, Elisabeth. "Typus der Heilsgeschichte oder Opfer morbider Gesellschaftsordnung? Ein Forschungsbericht zum Schuldproblem in Hartmanns *Gregorius* (1950–1971)." *Euphorion* 68: 42–80.

1974. Huby, Michel. "Adaptation courtoise et société ou 'La réalité dépasse la fiction.'" *Etudes Germaniques* 29: 289–301.

1974. Müller, Karl Friedrich. *Hartmann von Aue und die Herzöge von Zähringen*. Lahr: Schauenburg.

1974. Nölle, Marie. *Formen der Darstellung in Hartmanns Iwein*. Bern: Lang.

1974. Wiehl, Peter. *Die Redeszene als episches Strukturelement in den Erec- und Iwein-Dichtungen Hartmanns von Aue und Chrestiens de Troyes*. Munich: Fink.

1975. Gewehr, Wolf. *Hartmanns Klage-Büchlein im Lichte der Frühscholastik*. Göppingen: Kümmerle.

1975. Lewis, Robert E. *Symbolism in Hartmann's Iwein*. Göppingen: Kümmerle.

1976. Kalinke, Marianne. "*Vorhte* in Hartmanns *Erec*." *Amsterdamer Beiträge zur älteren Germanistik* 11: 67–80.

1977. Fourquet, Jean. "Les adaptations allemandes de romans chevalresques français." *Etudes Germaniques* 32: 97–107.

1977. Liebertz-Grün, Ursula. *Zur Soziologie des amour courtois: Umrisse der Forschung*. Heidelberg: Winter.

1978. Kuttner, Ursula. *Das Erzählen des Erzählten: eine Studie zum Stil in Hartmans Erec und Iwein*. Bonn: Bouvier.

1978a. Mertens, Volker. *Gregorius Eremita: eine Lebensform des Adels bei Hartmann von Aue in ihrer Problematik und ihrer Wandlung in der Rezeption*. Munich: Artemis.

1978b. Mertens, Volker. *Laudine: Soziale Problematik im Iwein Hartmanns von Aue*. Berlin: Schmidt.

1978. Ó Riain-Raedel, Dagmar. *Untersuchungen zur mythischen Struktur der mittelhochdeutschen Artusepen*. Berlin: Schmidt.

1978. Steinle, Gisela. *Hartmann von Aue, Kennzeichen durch Bezeichnen: Zur Verwendung der Personenbezeichnungen in seinen epischen Werken*. Bonn: Bouvier.

1979. Borck, Karl Heinz. "Nû ist sie vrî als ich dâ bin: Bemerkungen zu Hartmanns *Armen Heinrich* v.1497." *Medium Aevum deutsch. Beiträge zur deutschen Literatur des hohen und späten Mittelalters. Festschrift für Kurt Ruh zum 65, Geburtstag*. Ed. Dietrich Huschenbett et al. Tübingen: Niemeyer. 37–50.

1979. Herlem-Prey, Brigitte. *Le Gregorius et la Vie de saint Gregoire: determination de la source de Hartmann von Aue a partir de l'étude comparative integrale des textes*. Göppingen: Kümmerle.

1979. Hirschberg, Dagmar. "Zur Struktur von Hartmanns *Gregorius*." *Befund und Deutung: zum Verhältnis von Empirie und Interpretation in Sprach- und Literaturwissenschaft*. Eds. Klaus Grubmüller et al. Tübingen: Niemeyer. 240–67.

1979. Kraft, Karl-Friedrich O. *Iweins Triuwe: zu Ethos und Form der Aventiurenfolge in Hartmanns "Iwein": eine Interpretation*. Amsterdam: Rodopi.

1979. Ott, Norbert H., and Wolfgang Walliczek. "Bildprogramm und Textstruktur: Anmerkungen zu den *Iwein* Zyklen auf Rodeneck und in Schmalkalden." *Deutsche Literatur im Mittelalter: Kontakte und Perspektiven: Hugo Kuhn zum Gedenken*. Ed. Christoph Cormeau. Stuttgart: Metzler. 473–500.

1979. Pretzel, Ulrich. "Zum Prolog von Hartmanns *Gregorius* mit einem Exkurs über einen Sondergebrauch von mhd. *ein*." *Ulrich Pretzel: Kleine Schriften*. Ed. Wolfgang Bachofer. Berlin: Schmidt.

1979. Schweikle, Günther. "Der Stauferhof und die mittelhochdeutsche Lyrik, im besonderen zur Reinmar-Walther Fehde und zu Hartmanns *herre*." *Stauferzeit: Geschichte, Literatur, Kunst: [Ergebnis der Karlsruher Staufertagung 1977]*. Eds. Rüdiger Krohn, Bernd Thum, and Peter Wapnewski. Stuttgart: Klett.

1979. Thomas, J. W. Introduction. *Iwein*. By Hartmann von Aue. Trans. J. W. Thomas. Lincoln: University of Nebraska Press.

1979. Zutt, Herta. *König Artus, Iwein, der Löwe: die Bedeutung des gesprochenen Worts in Hartmanns Iwein.* Tübingen: Niemeyer.

1980. Arndt, Paul H. *Der Erzähler bei Hartmann von Aue: Formen und Funktionen seines Hervortretens und seiner Äußerungen.* Göppingen: Kümmerle.

1981. Grosse, Siegfried. "Die Variationen der Minne in den Dichtungen Hartmanns von Aue." *Interpretation und Edition deutscher Texte.* Eds. Kathryn Smits, Werner Besch, and Victor Lange. Schmidt: Berlin. 26–38.

1981. Smits, Kathryn. "Enite als christliche Ehefrau." *Interpretation und Edition Deutscher Texte des Mittelalters.* Eds. Kathryn Smits, Werner Besch, and Victor Lange. Berlin: Schmidt. 13–25.

1982. Henne, Hermann. *Herrschaftsstruktur, historischer Prozess und epische Handlung: sozialgeschichtliche Untersuchungen zum 'Gregorius' und 'Armen Heinrich' Hartmanns von Aue.* Göppingen: Kümmerle.

1982. Kratins, Ojars. *The dream of chivalry: a study of Chretien de Troyes's Yvain and Hartmann von Aue's Iwein.* Washington: University Press of America.

1982. Thomas, J. W. Introduction. *Erec.* By Hartmann von Aue. Trans. by J. W. Thomas. Lincoln: University of Nebraska Press.

1982. Wells, David A. "Die Ikonographie von Daniel IV und der Wahnsinn des Löwenritters." *Interpretation und Edition deutscher Texte des Mittelalters.* Eds. Kathryn Smits, Werner Besch, and Victor Lange. Berlin: Schmidt. 39–57.

1983. Brackert, Helmut. Afterword. *Minnesang: Mittelhochdeutscher Text und Übertragung.* Ed. and Trans. Helmut Brackert. Frankfurt a.M.: Fischer. 259–76.

1983. Fischer, Hubertus. *Ehre, Hof und Abenteuer in Hartmanns Iwein: Vorarbeiten zu einer historischen Poetik des höfischen Epos.* Munich: Fink.

1983. Plate, Bernward, ed. *Gregorius auf dem Stein: Frühneuhochdeutsche Prosa (15.Jh.) nach dem mittelhochdeutschen Versepos Hartmanns von Aue/Die Legende (Innsbruck UB Cod.631), der Text aus dem 'Heiligen Leben' und die sogenannte Redaktion.* Darmstadt: Wissenschaftliche Buchgesellschaft.

1983. Steiner, Gertraud. *Das Abenteuer der Regression: eine Untersuchung zur phantasmagorischen Wiederkehr der 'verlorenen Zeit' in Erec.* Göppingen: Kümmerle.

1983. Voß, Rudolf. *Die Artusepik Hartmanns von Aue: Untersuchungen zum Wirklichkeitsbegriff und zur Ästhetik eines literarischen Genres im Kräftefeld von soziokulturellen Normen und christlicher Anthropologie.* Cologne: Böhlau.

1984. Asher, John. "Motivverdoppelung im *Armen Heinrich.*" *Festschrift für Siegfried Grosse.* Eds. Werner Besch et al. Kümmerle: Göppingen. 313–24.

1984. Kern, Peter. "Reflexe des literarischen Gesprächs über Hartmanns *Erec.*" *Artusrittertum im späten Mittelalter: Ethos und Ideologie: Vorträge des Symposiums der deutschen Sektion der Internationalen Artusgesellschaft vom 10. bis 13. November 1983 im Schloß Rauischholzhausen (Universität Giessen).* Ed. Friedrich Wolfzettel. Giessen: Schmitz. 126–37.

1984. McConeghy, Patrick. Introduction. *Iwein.* By Hartmann von Aue. Ed. Trans. Patrick McConeghy. New York: Garland.

1984. Reusner, Ernst von. "Hartmanns Lyrik." *Germanisch Romanische Monatsschrift* 34: 8–28.

1984. Schwarz, Werner. "Free will in Hartmann's *Gregorius.*" *Beiträge zur mittelalterlichen Literatur.* Ed. Peter Ganz. Amsterdam: Rodopi. 25–44.

1985. Buschinger, Danielle. "Das Inzest-Motiv in der mittelalterlichen Literatur." *Psychologie in der Mediävistik.* Ed. Jürgen Kühnel. Kümmerle: Göppingen. 107–40.

1985. Cormeau, Christoph, and Wilhelm Störmer. *Hartmann von Aue: Epoche, Werk, Wirkung.* Munich: Beck.

1985. Krause, Burckhardt. "Zur Psychologie von Kommunikation und Interaktion: Zu Iweins 'Wahnsinn.'" *Psychologie in der Mediävistik.* Ed. Jürgen Kühnel. Goppingen: Kümmerle.

1985. Kühnel, Jürgen. "Ödipus und Gregorius." *Psychologie in der Mediävistik.* Ed. Jürgen Kühnel. Kümmerle: Göppingen. 141–70.

1985. Rautenberg, Ursula. *Das Volksbuch vom armen Heinrich: Studien zur Rezeption Hartmanns von Aue im 19. Jahrhundert und zur Wirkungsgeschichte der Übersetzung Wilhelm Grimms.* Berlin: Schmidt.

1985. Schmitt, Wolfram. "Der Wahnsinn in der Literatur des Mittelalters am Beispiel des *Iwein* Hartmanns von Aue." *Psychologie in der Mediävistik: gesammelte Beiträge des Steinheimer Symposions.* Eds. Jürgen Kühnel et al. Göppingen: Kümmerle.

1985. Steiner, Gertraud. "Unbeschreiblich weiblich: Zur mythischen Rezeption von Hartmanns *Iwein.*" *Psychologie in der Mediävistik.* Ed. Jürgen Kühnel. Kümmerle: Göppingen. 243–57.

1985. Trimborn, Karin. *Syntaktisch-stilistische Untersuchungen zu Chretiens Yvain and Hartmanns Iwein.* Berlin: Schmidt.

1986. Fisher, Rodney. "Räuber, Riesen und die Stimme der Vernunft in Hartmann's und Chrétien's *Erec.*" *Deutsche Vierteljahrschrift* 60: 353–74.

1986. Kaplowitt, Stephen J. *The ennobling power of love in the medieval German lyric.* Chapel Hill: UNC Press.

1986. Tobler, Eva. "Ancilla Domini: Marianische Aspekte in Hartmanns *Erec.*" *Euphorion* 80: 427–38.

1987. Giesa, Gerhard. *Märchenstrukturen und Archetypen in den Artusepen Hartmanns von Aue.* Göppingen: Kümmerle.

1987. Keller, Thomas. Introduction. *Erec.* By Hartmann von Aue. Trans. Thomas Keller. New York: Garland Press.

1987. Könneker, Barbara. *Hartmann von Aue: Der arme Heinrich.* Frankfurt: Diesterweg.

1987. McConeghy, Patrick M. "Womens' Speech and Silence in Hartmann von Aue's *Erec.*" *Publications of the Modern Language Association of America* 102: 771–83.

1987. Resler, Michael. Introduction. *Erec.* By Hartmann von Aue. Trans. Michael Resler. Philadelphia: University of Pennsylvania Press.

1987. Schnyder, André. "Forsche Ritter und fromme Ehefrau: Die Rezeption von Hartmanns *Erec* bei Christian Stecher." *Euphorion* 81: 298–314.

1988. Ehrismann, Otfried. "Laudine — oder Hartmanns *Iwein* postmodern" *Sammlung, Deutung, Wertung: Ergebnisse, Probleme, Tendenzen und Perspektiven philologischer Arbeit . . . offerts à Wolfgang Spiewok à l'occasion de son soixantième anniversaire.* Ed. Danielle Buschinger. Picardie: Centre des Etudes medievales. 91–100.

1988. Firestone, Ruth. "Boethian order in Hartmann's *Erec* and *Iwein.*" *Essays in Literature* 15: 117–30.

1988. *Hartmann von Aue, Changing Perspectives: London Hartmann Symposium, 1985.* Ed. Timothy McFarland and Sylvia Ranawake. Göppingen: Kümmerle.

1988. Heinen, Hubert. "Irony and Confession in Hartmanns *Sît ich den sumer* (MF 205,1)." *Monatshefte* 80: 416–29.

1988. Margetts, John. "Observations on the Representation of Female Attractiveness in the Works of Hartmann von Aue with Special Reference to *Der arme Heinrich.*" In 1988: *Hartmann von Aue, Changing Perspectives: London Hartmann Symposium, 1985.* 199–210.

1988. Mertens, Volker. "*Factus est per clericum miles cythereus:* Überlegungen zu Entstehungs- und Wirkungsbedingungen von Hartmanns *Klage-Büchlein.*" In 1988: *Hartmann von Aue, Changing Perspectives: London Hartmann Symposium, 1985.* 1–20.

1988. Ranawake, Sylvia. "Erec's *verligen* and the sin of sloth." In 1988: *Hartmann von Aue, Changing Perspectives: London Hartmann Symposium, 1985.* 93–116.

1988. Sayce, Olive. "Romance Elements in the Lyrics of Hartmann von Aue." In 1988: *Hartmann von Aue, Changing Perspectives: London Hartmann Symposium, 1985.* 53–64.

1988. Schulte-Sasse, Jochen. "The Concept of Literary Criticism in German Romanticism." *A History of German Literary Criticism.* Ed. Peter Uwe Hohendahl. Lincoln: University of Nebraska Press. 99–178.

1988. Seiffert, Leslie. "On the Language of Sovereignty, Deference and Solidarity: The Surrender of the Accusing Lover in Hartmann's *Klage.*" In 1988: *Hartmann von Aue, Changing Perspectives: London Hartmann Symposium, 1985.* 21–52.

1988. Sparre, Sulamith. *Todessehnsucht un Erlösung: Tristan und Armer Heinrich in der deutschen Literatur um 1900.* Göppingen: Kümmerle.

1989. Clark, Susan. *Hartmann von Aue: Landscapes of Mind.* Houston: Rice University Press.

1989. Czerwinski, Peter. *Der Glanz der Abstraktion: Frühe Formen von Reflexivität im Mittelalter* (Frankfurt: Campus).

1989. Ehrismann, Otfried. "Höfisches Leben und Individualität: Hartmanns *Erec.*" *Aspekte der Germanistik: Festschrift für Hans-Friedrich Rosenfeld zum 90. Geburtstag.* Ed. Walter Tauber. Göppingen: Kümmerle. 99–122.

1989. Graf, Michael. *Liebe, Zorn, Trauer, Adel: die Pathologie in Hartmann von Aues Iwein: eine Interpretation auf medizinhistorischer Basis.* New York: Lang.

1989. Katzenmeier, Ursula. *Das Schachspiel des Mittelalters als Strukturierungsprinzip der Erec-Romane.* Heidelberg: Winter.

1989. Pastré, Jean-Marc. "Le *Gregorius,* la croisade et la chronologie des oeuvres de Hartmann von Aue." *La croisade: realites et fictions: actes du colloques d'Amiens, 18–22 mars 1987.* Ed. Danielle Buschinger. Kümmerle: Göppingen. 183–92.

1989. Kathryn Smits, "Bemerkungen zu den Motiven der Diesseitsflucht und Eheflucht im *Armen Heinrich* Hartmanns von Aue." *La croisade: Realites et fictions.* Ed. Danielle Buschinger. Kümmerle: Göppingen.

1989. Spiewok, Wolfgang. "Zum *Gregorius* Hartmanns von Aue." *Mittelalter-Studien II.* Göppingen: Kümmerle. 128–37.

1989. Wand, Christiane. *Wolfram von Eschenbach und Hartmann von Aue: Literarische Reaktionen auf Hartmann im Parzival*. Herne: Verlag für Wissenschaft und Kunst.

1990. Duckworth, David. "Heinrich and the Godless Life in Hartmann's Poem." *Mediaevistik* 3: 71–90.

1990. Willms, Eva. *Liebesleid und Sangeslust: Untersuchungen zur deutschen Liebeslyrik des späten 12. und frühen 13. Jahrhunderts*. Munich: Artemis.

1990. Wis, Marjatta. "Hartmann von Aue und *Vranken:* Zur Saladin-Crux im Kreuzlied MF 218.5." *Neuphilologische Mitteilungen* 91: 401–11.

1991. Dahlgrün, Corinna. *Hoc fac, et vives (LK 10,28)* — *Vor allen dingen minne got: theologische Reflexionen eines Laien im Gregorius und im Armen Heinrich Hartmanns von Aue*. Frankfurt: Lang.

1991. Jacobson, Evelyn M. "The unity of *wort* und *sinn:* Language as a theme and structural element in Hartmann's *Erec*." *Seminar* 27: 121–35.

1991. See, Geoffrey. "An examination of the hero in Hartmann's *Erec.*" *Seminar* 27: 39–54.

1991. Sterba, Wendy. "The question of Enite's transgression: Female voice and male gaze as determining factors in Hartmann's *Erec.*" *Women as protagonists and poets in the German Middle Ages: An anthology of feminist approaches to Middle High German literature*. Edited by Albrecht Classen. Göppingen: Kümmerle. 57–68.

1991. Schnell, Rüdiger. "Abaelards Gesinnungsethik und die Rechtsthematik in Hartmanns *Iwein.*" *Deutsche Vierteljahrschrift* 65: 15–69.

1991. Wis, Marjatta. "Hartmanns Connelant und Chrétiens Cligès." *Neuphilologische Mitteilungen* 92: 269–80.

1992. Kellermann, Karina. "*Exemplum* und *historia:* Zu poetologischen Traditionen in Hartmanns *Iwein.*" *Germanisch-Romanische Monatsschrift* 42: 1–27.

1992. Wailes, Stephen L. "Hartmann von Aue's stories of incest." *Journal for English and Germanic Philology* 91: 65–78.

1993. Quast, Bruno. "*Getriuwiu wandelunde:* Ehe und Minne in Hartmanns *Erec.*" *Zeitschrift für deutsches Altertum* 122: 162–80.

1994. Beutin, Heidi and Wolfgang Beutin. *Der Löwenritter in den Zeiten der Aufklärung: Gerhard Anton von Halems Iwein-Version "Ritter Twein," ein Beitrag zur dichterischen Mittelalter-Rezeption des 18. Jahrhunderts* (Göppingen: Kümmerle).

1994. Jackson, W.H. *Chivalry in Twelfth-Century Germany: The Works of Hartmann von Aue* (Cambridge: Brewer).

Reference works

Boggs, R.A. *Hartmann von Aue: lemmatisierte Konkordanz zum Gesamtwerk.* Nendeln: KTO Press, 1979.

Cormeau, Christoph. "Hartmann von Aue." *Die deutsche Literatur des Mittelalters: Verfasserlexikon.* Vol. 3. Ed. Kurt Ruh. Berlin: de Gruyter, 1987. 500–20.

Cormeau, Christoph and Wilhelm Störmer. *Hartmann von Aue: Epoche, Werk, Wirkung.* Munich: Beck, 1985.

Haase, Gudrun. *Die germanistische Forschung zum Erec Hartmanns von Aue.* Frankfurt: Lang, 1988.

Hasty, Will. "Hartmann von Aue." *German Writers and Works of the High Middle Ages: 1170–1270.* Vol. 138 of the *Dictionary of Literary Biography.* Detroit: Bruccoli Clark Layman, 1994. 27–43.

Klemt, Ingrid. *Hartmann von Aue: Eine Zusammenstellung der über ihn und sein Werk von 1927 bis 1968 erschienenen Literatur.* Köln: Greven, 1968.

Neubuhr, Elfriede. *Bibliographie zu Hartmann von Aue.* Berlin: Schmidt, 1977.

Peter Wapnewski. *Hartmann von Aue.* Stuttgart: Metzler, 1962. Seventh edition: Stuttgart: Metzler, 1979.

Index

Abelard, 61, 94, 116
adaptation courtoise, 38, 53, 84, 110
Ambras Manuscript (Ambraser Heldenbuch), 12, 23, 36
Andreas Capellanus (*De amore*), 39
Arndt, Paul H., 12, 69, 112
Arthur (King), 19, 22, 36, 38, 42, 45–47, 49–50, 79, 81, 87, 89–93, 95, 97
Arthurian Literature, 4, 9–11, 13, 17–20, 28, 36, 40–41, 47, 50, 55–56, 65–66, 70, 81, 83–86, 90, 97, 108–114
Ascalon (in *Iwein*), 79, 81, 83, 86–92
Asceticism, 25–26, 64
Asher, John, 71, 113
Augustine, St. (conception of sin), 49, 61, 73, 89, 92

Bartels, Adolf, 4, 104
Barthel, Karl, 21, 29, 37, 39, 41, 43, 56–57, 70, 71, 82, 85, 103
Bede, 55, 73
Benecke, Georg Friedrich, 1, 4, 102
Bennholdt-Thomsen, 54, 107
Bernard of Clairvaux, 73
Bernard of Thiron, 64
Bertold IV/Bertold V (of the Zähringer), 16
Beutin, Heidi, 2–3, 116
Beutin, Wolfgang, 2–3, 116
bipartite structure (*Doppelwegstruktur*), 25, 40, 42, 56, 81, 86–87
Blattmann, Ekkehard, 28, 34, 109
Bodmer, Johann Jakob, 1–3, 101
Boethius (*Consolatio Philosophiae*), 45
Boggs, R.A., 117
Book of Taliesin, 80
Boor, Helmut de, 70, 77, 85, 106
Borck, Karl Heinz, 77–78, 109, 111
Borst, Arno, 64, 109
Brackert, Helmut, 27–28, 112
Breitinger, Johann Jakob, 1–3, 101
Brody, Saul N., 72, 110
Buck, Timothy, 73, 108

Bürck, Emma, 21, 105
Buschinger, Danielle, 54, 113–115

Caesarius of Heisterbach, 71
Carne, Eva-Maria, 48, 109
Chamisso, Adalbert, 69
Chrétien de Troyes, 6, 14–15, 17, 34, 36–40, 42–44, 46, 80–84, 86, 90–91, 93, 95–96, 114, 116
Clark, Susan, 9, 13, 27, 45–46, 65, 91, 94, 97, 115
Cluniac Reform, 9, 65
Connelant (Ikonium), 19, 105, 116
Constantine (Roman Emperor), 72
Constantinus Africanus, 93
Cormeau, Christoph, 61–62, 65–66, 73–76, 102, 105–111
Cormeau, Christoph (with Wilhelm Störmer), xi, 15, 18, 20–21, 34, 37, 39, 54–55, 68, 72, 79, 83, 85, 113, 117
Cramer, Thomas, 44, 80, 89, 92, 108–109
Crusades, 13, 16–19, 21, 30–35, 55
Czerwinski, Peter, 49–50, 93, 115

Dahlgrün, Corinna, 56, 66, 73, 116
Der jüngere Titurel, 11
development (in Hartmann's literary career), 18, 21–22, 32–35, 78; (of the heroes), xii, xiii, 39, 41–43, 46–51, 80, 84, 86–87, 90, 92–95
Die Große Heidelberger Liederhandschrift (Manesse Codex), 27, 101
Die Kleine Heidelberger Liederhandschrift, 27
Die Weingartner Liederhandschrift, 27
Dittmann, Wolfgang, 61–62, 108
Dorst, Tankred, xi
Drube, Herbert W., 82, 105
dualism, 6, 25–26, 63, 66–67, 73–78, 96, 105, 110
Duckworth, David, 73, 116

120 INDEX

Eggers, Hans, 7, 56, 71, 106
Ehrismann, Gustav, 25, 105
Ehrismann, Otfried, 50, 94, 98, 114–115
Eleanor of Aquitaine, 52
Elias, Norbert, 28, 106
Endres, Rolf, 73, 108
Enlightenment, 2–3
Erdmann, Oskar, 6, 104
Erex (Old Norse), 37
Eroms, Hans-Werner, 22, 47, 109

Fechter, Werner, 71, 74, 106
Fimery, Joseph L., 13, 104
Firdûsîs Book of Kings (Persian), 53
Firestone, Ruth, 45, 114
Fischer, Hubertus, 13, 46, 49, 80, 92–93, 95, 98, 112
Fisher, Rodney, 43, 45, 91, 114
Floire et Blancheflor, 25
Förster, Wendelin, 82, 103
Fourquet, Jean, 19, 38, 71, 84, 105, 107, 110
Frederick I (Barbarossa), 16–17, 19
Frederick the Great (of Prussia), 2
Freidank, 73
Frenzel, Elizabeth, 69, 106
Frenzel, Herbert A., 69, 106
Freud, Sigmund, 49, 53
Friedrich von Hausen, 28

Gärtner, Gustaf, 6, 82, 85–86, 103
Gauriel von Muntabel, 11, 36
Gawein, Sir (in the Arthurian works), 81, 87, 91
genre, xii, 11, 25, 28, 34, 55–56, 69–70, 76–78, 113
Geoffrey of Monmouth, 80.
Gereint (Mabinogion), 37
German (attitude, spirit, values), 3–6, 37–38, 69, 82–83, 85
Geruntius, 39
Gervinus, Georg G., 3–4, 39, 69, 73, 103
Gewehr, Wolf, 25–26, 110
Gierach, Erich, 9, 102, 105
Giesa, Gerhard, 82, 114
Gleim, Johann Wilhelm Ludwig, 1
Goebel, K. Dieter, 63–64, 110
Goedeke, Karl, 37, 85, 103
Goethe, Johann Wolfgang von, 13
Gododdin Cycle, 80
Goldast, Melchior Haiminsfeld, 1
Gössmann, Elisabeth, 59, 63, 110
Gothic architecture, 7, 9

Gottfried von Straßburg, 11–12, 18, 70, 79, 105, 107
Gottsched, Johann Christoph, 2–3
gradualism, 26, 63, 75–78, 96, 110
Graf, Michael, 93, 115
Grimm, The Brothers, 1, 4–5, 17, 69–71, 102
Grimm, Wilhelm, 113
Grosse, Siegfried, 20, 21, 26, 107, 112–113
guilt (*Schuld*), 33, 36, 41, 43, 47–49, 53, 57, 59–66, 73, 84, 88–89, 92–93, 106–107, 109–110

Haase, Gudrun, 117
Hagen, Paul, 6, 104
Halbach, Kurt, 13, 83, 106
Halem, Gerhard Anton von, 2, 116
Hartmann von Aue:
biographical attempts 7, 12, 29, 32, 105–106, 117; education 13–14, 26; family history 16–17; homeland 14–15; participation in crusade(s) 17–18; patron(s) 14–17, 34, 55, 68, 77, 85, 96; self-references 12–13; visual representations of 12, 15–16
Hartmann von Aue, Works by:
Der arme Heinrich xi, 1–5, 13–14, 16, 19–21, 52, 56, 60, 63, 66–67, *68–78*, 88, 101–102, 104, 106–107, 109–110, 114
Erec xi, 1, 8, 12, 18–21, 23, 25, *36–51*, 52, 66, 78–80, 82, 84–85, 87, 90–91, 93, 101–106, 108–117
Gregorius xi, 1, 18, 20, 22, *52–67*, 76, 78, 84, 91, 102–104, 106–113, 115–116
Iwein xi, 1–2, 5–6, 14, 18–21, 23, 36, 39–40, 47, 49, 69, 78, *79–95*, 102–104, 105–113
Klage (Büchlein) xi, 1, 14, 20, *23–27*, 28–30, 32–33, 36, 55, 66, 103, 108, 110, 115
Lyrics, xiii, 1, 6, 12–13, 21, 23, *27–35*, 55, 101, 114, 115
Hasty, Will, 117
Hatto, A.T., 11, 107
Hauck, Albert, 58, 105
Haupt, Moriz, 1, 23–24, 27, 31, 36, 101–102
Hauptmann, Gerhart, 69
Heinen, Hubert, 35, 114
Heinrich VI, 17

Heinrich von dem Türlîn, 11, 14, 18, 36, 79
Heinrich von Morungen, 28
Heinrich von Veldeke, 24
Heinze, Joachim, xi
Heinze, Norbert, 7, 21, 110
Heinzel, Richard, 13, 103, 104
Henne, Hermann, 65–66, 71, 75, 112
Henrici, Emil, 6, 103
Henry II (Plantagenet), 52
Herlem-Prey, Brigitte, 52, 111
Hessenhof (Iwein fresco), 79
Heyne, Wilhelm, 6, 104
Hirschberg, Dagmar, 56, 111
Historia Britonum, 80
Hölty, Ludwig Christoph Heinrich, 1
Hrabanus Maurus, 73
Huby, Michel, 38, 84, 110
Huch, Ricarda, 69
Humanism, 1

Ittenbach, Max, 7, 105
Ivan (Swedish), 80
Ivens Saga (Old Norse), 80

Jackson, W.H., 26–27, 35, 46, 56, 66, 77, 95, 116
Jacobson, Evelyn M., 44–45, 91, 116
Jantzen, Hermann, 38, 105
Jeske, Georg Gustav August, 6, 82, 104
joie de la curt (episode in *Erec*), 38, 41, 42, 44, 50
Jong, Jan de, 13, 108
Jungian psychology, 82

Kafka, Franz, xi
Kaiser, Erich, 69, 108
Kaiser, Gert, 28, 90, 110
Kalinke, Marianne, 44
Kalogreant, Sir (figure in *Iwein*), 81, 86–87, 92
Kant, Immanuel, 92, 98
Kaplowitt, Stephen, 28, 35, 114
Katzenmeier, Ursula, 43, 115
Kay, Sir (in the Arthurian works), 44, 87
Keller, Thomas, 14, 39, 42, 114
Kellermann, Karina, 95, 116
Kern, Peter, 36, 113
Kildisch Arslan, 19
King, Kenneth C., 60–61, 107
Kleiber, H., 37–39, 43, 104
Klemt, Ingrid, 109, 117
Konrad Fleck, 11

Konrad von Würzburg, 11, 72
Köhler, Erich, 28, 90, 109–110
Könneker, Barbara, 69, 71–72, 75, 77, 114
Kraft, Karl-Friedrich O., 91, 111
Kramer, Hans-Peter, 83, 109
Kratins, Ojars, 91, 112
Kraus, Carl von, 23, 101, 104
Krause, Burckhardt, 92–93, 113
krutzouber (in the *klage*), 14, 28
Kudrun 4
Kuhn, Hugo, 8, 18, 25, 33, 40–42, 46–48, 59, 71, 88, 92, 96, 98, 105–111
Kühnel, Jürgen, 65–66, 113
Kuttner, Ursula, 13, 111

Lachmann, Karl, 1, 4–5, 7, 21, 27, 31, 82, 86, 101–102
Langer, Theodor B., 6, 105
Laudine (figure in *Iwein*), 34, 79, 82–83, 85, 87–95, 98, 111, 114
lay religiosity, 66
Lewis, Robert E., 90–91, 110
Liebertz-Grün, Ursula, 28, 110
Linke, Hansjürgen, 7–8, 21, 39, 109
lion (in *Iwein*), 80, 85–87, 89–90
Lunete (in *Iwein*), 81, 87

McConeghy, Patrick, 45, 47, 79, 84, 87, 113–114
Mabinogion, 37, 80
Machule, Paul, 54, 104
Manichaeism, 75
Mann, Thomas, xi, 69, 108
manuscripts, xii, 5, 12, 15–17, 20, 23, 27, 36, 52–54, 68, 79.
Margetts, John, 76, 114
marriage, 16, 19, 38, 42–43, 45–46, 48, 63, 68, 76–77, 91
Martin, E., 6, 104
Marxism, 93
Maximilian I, 23
Meinloh von Sevelingen, 28
Mertens, Volker, 14–17, 26, 52–53, 55–56, 64–65, 68, 91, 111, 115
Meyer, Conrad Ferdinand, 69
Minne (Minnedienst), 24–26, 28, 30, 32–35, 42, 55, 83, 101, 103, 112, 116
Minnesang, 1, 15, 18, 27, 29, 32–35, 101, 106, 109–110, 112
ministeriales (social class), 14, 16, 90, 96

Monsterberg-Mückenau, Silvius von, 6, 103
moralism, xi, xiii, 13, 26, 30, 45–46, 50, 72, 77, 83, 88, 91–92, 94–96, 98, 108
Moser, Hugo, 27, 101
Muth, Richard V., 6, 103
Müller, Karl Friedrich, 14, 16, 110
Myller, Christoph Heinrich, 2, 102

Nagel, Bert, 73, 106
Napoleon, 5
Napoleonic Years, 3, 69
National Socialism, 83
nationalism, 3, 5, 10, 38, 69, 83–84, 97
Naumann, Hans, 6, 104
Neubuhr, Elfriede, 117
Neumann, Friedrich, 20, 107
Nibelungenlied 3–5, 69
Nobel, Hildegard, 59–60, 107
Nölle, Marie, 90–91, 110
Nordmeyer, Henry W., 8, 106

Ó Riain-Raedel, Dagmar, 40, 81, 111
objectivity, 5–10, 31, 33–35, 41, 46, 48–50, 62, 66, 87, 91–92, 94–95, 97–98
Ohly, Walter, 59, 72, 107
Okken, Lambertus, 6, 109
Ott, Norbert H. (with Wolfgang Walliczek), 80, 111
Otto IV, 18
Owen (Son of Uriens), 80
Owen, Heinricus de, 17
Owen and Luned (*Mabinogion*) 80

Paracelsus, 72
Pastré, Jean-Marc, 18, 20, 115
Patristic Literature, 8, 25, 48, 55
Paul, Hermann, 17, 102, 104
Pawel, Ernst, xi
Peetz, Helmut, 6, 104
penance (*Sühne*), 49, 53–62, 64–65, 84
Peter of Lombard, 58, 62
Peter of Poitiers, 58
Peters, Ursula, 28, 110
Pfeiffer, Franz, 5, 39, 103
Philip von Schwaben, 18
philology (textual criticism), xii, 1, 5–7
Piquet, Felix, 23–25, 104
Plate, Bernward, 53, 56, 112
Pleier, der, 11, 79
Pliny, 71
plot, xii, 7–9, 40–42, 50, 87, 90–92, 98
Prawer, Siegbert, xi
Pretzel, Ulrich, 54, 111

Propp, V. 82

Quast, Bruno, 46, 48, 116

Ranawake, Sylvia, 43–44, 114–115
Rautenberg, Ursula, 69, 74, 113
Reinmar, 27–28, 34, 111
Resler, Michael, 37–38, 42, 47, 114
Reusner, Ernst von, 34, 113
Ried, Hans (of Bozen), 23, 36
Robert of Arbrissel, 64
Rodeneck Castle (Iwein fresco), 79
Romanticism (Romantics), 2–6, 9, 13, 21, 29, 31, 34, 57, 69–71, 98, 115
Rosenhagen, Gustav, 19, 105
Rudolf von Ems, 11, 79
Rudolf von Fenis, 28
Ruh, Kurt, 46, 48, 88–89, 94, 108, 111, 117

Sachsenspiegel, 24
Saladin, 17–18, 116
Saran, Franz, 6, 13, 23, 28, 31–33, 86, 103–104
Sayce, Olive, 28, 115
Scherer, Wilhelm, 4, 21, 36, 53, 56, 69, 85, 103
Schieb, Gabriele, 59–60, 106
Schirokauer, Arno, 20, 73–76, 101, 106
Schmid, Ludwig, 6, 15, 29–30, 35, 103
Schmitt, Wolfram, 93, 113
Schnell, Rüdiger, 94, 116
Schnyder, André, 36, 114
Scholasticism 9, 25–26, 48, 61–62, 64, 90, 93, 107, 110
Schönbach, Anton E., 6, 24–25, 54, 56–59, 61, 72, 82, 84, 90, 104
Schottmann, Hans, 52, 108
Schreyer, Hermann, 6, 15, 29–31, 35, 103
Schröder, Joachim, 22, 47, 87, 109
Schröder, Werner, 20, 107
Schroeder, Edward, 6, 104
Schulte-Sasse, Jochen, 2–3, 115
Schultz, Alwin, 6, 103
Schwabenspiegel, 25
Schwarz, Werner, 61, 66, 108
Schweikle, Günther, 16
Schwietering, Julius, 55, 105
See, Geoffrey, 45, 116
Seiffert, Leslie, 25, 76, 107, 115
Seigfried, H., 62–63, 109
Selisch, Adolf, 6, 103
Smits, Kathryn, 48, 74, 112, 115

Sophocles, 53, 69
Sparnaay, Hendrik, 7, 15–16, 18–19, 21, 24–25, 28, 32–34, 37, 39- 40, 52–55, 68, 70, 72–74, 80–81, 83–84, 86, 88, 90, 105–106, 108
Sparre, Sulamith, 69–70, 115
Spiewok, Wolfgang, 65–66, 114–115
Steiner, Gertraud, 49–50, 93–94, 98, 112–113
Steinle, Gisela, 47, 111
Sterba, Wendy, 47, 116
Störmer, Wilhelm (with Christoph Cormeau), xi, 15, 18, 20–21, 34, 37, 39, 54–55, 68, 72, 79, 83, 85, 113, 117
structure xii, 5, 7–9, 25, 39–43, 48, 55–56, 63, 65, 71, 81, 85–87, 91, 98
style, 1, 6, 21, 55, 83–85, 95
subjectivity, 5–6, 8–10, 29, 32, 35, 41, 46, 61–62, 66, 91, 94–95, 97–98
Sylvester (Legend of Pope), 72
symbolism 7, 25, 43–44, 46, 54, 56–57, 59, 70, 72, 74–75, 86- 87, 89, 91, 93, 108, 110

Tardel, Hermann, 69, 104
Tax, Petrus, 43, 47, 101, 108
Tervooren, Helmut, 27, 101
Thomas, J.W., 11, 13, 15, 21, 47, 87, 89, 111–112
Thomasîn von Zerclaere, 73
Tobin, Frank. J., 57, 62–63, 74, 76, 110
Tobler, Eva, 44, 114
Trimborn, Karin, 38, 83–84, 114

Ulrich Füetrer, 80
Ulrich von Türheim, 11
Ulrich von Liechtenstein, 29–30

Vatalis of Savigny, 64
verligen (theme in *Erec*), 36, 42–44, 46, 50, 87, 115
Verweyen, Theodor, 75–76, 109
Vie du pape Grégoire 52, 108
Visio Fulberti 23, 25
Vos, Bert John, 6, 104
Voß, Johann Heinrich, 1
Voß, Rudolf, 8, 38, 46–48, 50, 80, 92–95, 98, 113

Wagner, Richard, 4
Wailes, Stephen L., 76, 116
Walliczek, Wolfgang (with Norbert H. Ott), 80, 111

Walther von der Vogelweide, 12, 27, 33–34, 111
Wand, Christane, 11, 116
Wapnewski, Peter, xi, 24–26, 33–35, 37–38, 52–56, 60, 63, 65, 72–74, 80, 83, 88–89, 92, 94, 107, 111, 117
Wehrli, Max, 89, 93, 109
Wells, David A., 80, 112
Wespersbühl, House of, 16
Wiehl, Peter, 8, 21, 38, 110
Wigamur 11
William Firmat, 64
William of St. Thierry, 73
Willms, Eva, 35, 116
Willson, Harold B., 60, 74, 107
Wilmanns, Wilhelm, 31, 103
Wis, Marjatta, 19, 21, 24, 116
Wisniewski, Roswitha, 24–26, 108
Witte, A., 13, 105
Wirnt von Grafenberg, 11
Wlislocki, Heinrich von, 71, 103
Wolf, Alois, 52, 61, 108
Wolfram von Eschenbach, 3–4, 11, 18, 36–37, 40, 42, 79, 86, 96, 104, 116

Ywain and Gawain (Middle English) 80

Zähringer, House of, 14–17
Zuntz, Günther, 53, 61, 106
Zutt,, Herta, 91, 101, 112
Zwierzina, Konrad, 6, 20, 55, 104